Strategies for the Threshold #5

Dealing with Leviathan:
Spirit of Retaliation

Anne Hamilton

Dealing with Leviathan: Spirit of Retaliation

Strategies for the Threshold #5

© Anne Hamilton 2020

Published by Armour Books

P. O. Box 492, Corinda QLD 4075

Cover Images: © Kevin Carden | Man holding up Bible to dragon;
© iloveotto | Canstockphoto;
© Diego Passadori |Unsplash: Brown wooden surface

Section Divider Image: © Cattallina | Dreamstime.com

Tabernacle Diagram: based on an original by Pearl | Lightstock.com

Interior Design and Typeset by Beckon Creative

ISBN: 978-1-925380-279

A catalogue record for this book is available from the National Library of Australia

Please note: the spelling, grammar and punctuation in this book are consistent with Australian language conventions.

All rights reserved. No part of this publication may be reproduced, stored in, or introduced into a retrieval system, or transmitted, in any form, or by any means (electronic, mechanical, photocopying, recording or otherwise) without the prior written permission of the publisher.

Strategies for the Threshold #5

Dealing with Leviathan:
Spirit of Retaliation

Anne Hamilton

Scripture quotations marked AKJV from The Authorized (King James) Version. Rights in the Authorized Version in the United Kingdom are vested in the Crown. Reproduced by permission of the Crown's patentee, Cambridge University Press.

Scripture quotations marked BSB are taken from the The Holy Bible, Berean Study Bible, BSB Copyright ©2016 by Bible Hub Used by Permission. All Rights Reserved Worldwide.

Scripture quotations marked CEV are taken from the Contemporary English Version® of the Bible. Copyright © 1995 American Bible Society. All rights reserved. Used by permission.

Scripture quotations marked ESV are taken from the ESV® Bible (The Holy Bible, English Standard Version®), copyright © 2001 by Crossway, a publishing ministry of Good News Publishers. Used by permission. All rights reserved.

Scripture quotations marked GWT are taken from GOD'S WORD®, a copyrighted work of God's Word to the Nations. Quotations are used by permission. Copyright 1995 by God's Word to the Nations. All rights reserved.

Scripture quotations marked HNV are taken from the Hebrew Names Version of the Bible. Public domain.

Scripture quotations marked ISV are taken from the Holy Bible: International Standard Version®. Copyright © 1996-forever by The ISV Foundation. All rights reserved internationally. Used by permission.

Scripture quotations marked KJV are taken from the King James Version of the Bible. Public domain.

Scripture quotations marked NAS are taken from the New American Standard Bible®, Copyright © 1960, 1962, 1963, 1968, 1971, 1972, 1973, 1975, 1977, 1995 by The Lockman Foundation. Used by permission. (www.Lockman.org)

Scripture quotations designated NET are from the NET Bible® copyright ©1996-2016 by Biblical Studies Press, L.L.C. http://netbible.com Scripture quoted by permission. All rights reserved.

Scripture quotations marked NHEB are taken from the New Heart English Bible. Public Domain.

Scripture quotations marked NIV are taken from the Holy Bible, New International Version®, NIV®. Copyright © 1973, 1978, 1984, 2011 by Biblica, Inc.™ Used by permission of Zondervan. All rights reserved worldwide. www.zondervan.com The "NIV" and "New International Version" are trademarks registered in the United States Patent and Trademark Office by Biblica, Inc.™.

Scripture quotations marked NKJV are taken from the New King James Version. Copyright © 1982 by Thomas Nelson, Inc. Used by permission. All rights reserved.

Scripture quotations marked NLT are taken from the Holy Bible, New Living Translation, copyright 1996, 2004. Used by permission of Tyndale House Publishers, Inc., Wheaton, Illinois 60189. All rights reserved.

Scripture quotations marked NRS are taken from New Revised Standard Version of the Bible, copyright 1952 [2nd edition, 1971] by the Division of Christian Education of the National Council of the Churches of Christ in the United States of America. Used by permission. All rights reserved.

Scripture quotations marked TLB are taken from The Living Bible copyright © 1971 by Tyndale House Foundation. Used by permission of Tyndale House Publishers Inc., Carol Stream, Illinois 60188. All rights reserved.

Other Books By

Anne Hamilton

In this series

Dealing with Python: Spirit of Constriction

Dealing with Ziz: Spirit of Forgetting

Name Covenant: Invitation to Friendship

Hidden in the Cleft: True and False Refuge

Devotional Theology series

God's Poetry: The Identity & Destiny Encoded in Your Name
God's Panoply: The Armour of God & the Kiss of Heaven
God's Pageantry: The Threshold Guardians & the Covenant Defender
God's Pottery: The Sea of Names & the Pierced Inheritance
God's Priority: World-Mending & Generational Testing
More Precious than Pearls (with *Natalie Tensen*)
As Resplendent As Rubies (with *Natalie Tensen*)
Spiritual Legal Rights (with *Janice Sergison*)

Jesus and the Healing of History Series

1 ***Like Wildflowers, Suddenly***
2 ***Bent World, Bright Wings***
3 ***Silk Shadows, Rings of Gold***
4 ***Where His Feet Pass***
5 ***The Singing Silence***

Thank you

Dell   Jim
James   Brian
Donna   Quang
Ben   Rebekah
Joy   Richard
Genevieve Rosemary
Brad   Sam
Ruth   Laurie
Waipatu Desiree
Janice Josephine
Joye   Janne
Kerry   Steve
Natalie David
Mike   Ina
Melissa Julie

Contents

Introduction		ix
1	**Remember the Battle**	1
2	**Seize the Day**	19
3	**Heavenly Courtier**	41
4	**Sight, Smell, Taste**	73
5	**Forensic Accounting**	97
6	**Chaos and Enchantment**	149
7	**Lines, Links, Land**	185
Appendix 1	Summary	213
Appendix 2	Honour and Dishonour	217
Appendix 3	Honouring Other	225
Appendix 4	The Number of a Man and also a Beast	227
Endnotes		241

Introduction

THIS BOOK WEAVES TOGETHER two different branches of knowledge: the theoretical and the experiential. As I've worked to understand how my personal encounters with Leviathan fit with the biblical description of it, I've read many books, watched many videos and listened to many audio presentations. Particularly in the audio presentations I noticed a peculiar phenomenon—about fifty minutes in, Leviathan arrived. It manifested as obviously present in the room when the speaker started a sudden rant. I've wondered if, in carelessly talking about this stunningly magnificent and immensely daunting creature, the speaker was actually inviting it to turn up.

So I have prayed very carefully over this book. Although it discusses Leviathan at length as well as several of the other threshold guardians, nothing I've written here constitutes an invitation for those spirits to manifest in any way as you progress through the book. I have also asked the Lord Jesus, through the power of His precious blood, to watch over the wording here and protect it from any twisting or distortion that Leviathan might hope would bring clouding to your mind or confusion to your spirit.

My experience of Leviathan is very different from that of other people. The main theme of this book in relation to it has, as far as I am aware, not been expressed by other writers or speakers to date. In addition, as I researched this topic for this book, I became aware of the strong possibility that the entity we call 'Leviathan' might also be hiding under another name in Scripture. However, so as not to muddle the distinctive characteristics applying to each particular identification, I have chosen to cover this issue in a companion book, *Dealing with Resheph: Spirit of Trouble*.

Like all my other books, this one has a numerical underlay. Each chapter is divided into sections and most of them are multiples of 111—the covenant number found in the mathematical structure of John 17—as well as multiples of 101, the number symbolising God's sustaining power.

My thanks once again to my mum, who has written some beautiful prayers for the end of each chapter. Many thanks also to those who told me their stories of discovering the roots of dishonour in their lives and then bravely gave me permission to use their testimonies as illustrations in these pages.

I pray that, as you read, the Father of our Lord Jesus Christ will sing over you with His protection. May you discern the wiles of the evil one and never let go of the hem of Jesus' garment as He arises on your life with healing in His wings.

Anne Hamilton
Brisbane, Australia 2020

1

Remember the Battle

I FIRST CAME TO HEAR ABOUT LEVIATHAN as a spirit of retaliation when I lived in a tiny town near the southern edge of the world. Only a drive of a couple of hours away is a windswept, sheep-dotted headland swirled by seas at the uttermost 'ends of the earth'. At least that's the view of the orthodox rabbis who are occasionally seen on the track, praying as they walk down towards the lighthouse.

The tiny township where I was living was a forestry centre encircled by mountains. Their lower slopes were the deep, mysterious green of pine plantations. Just a few years back, the town was used as a film location for a remake of the Disney feature, *Pete's Dragon*. It's no coincidence it was chosen to be a backdrop for a movie about a dragon. Some landscapes, as we shall see, are favourite haunts of the Leviathan spirit.

My first experience of hearing people talk openly about Leviathan was back in 2006. It influenced my entire perspective from that point on. It all began when I happened to be on the edge of a curious conversation. A group of people at an inter-church gathering were talking about a friend of theirs who'd been involved in high level spiritual warfare. 'It's over a year now,' one of them said. 'The doctors haven't been able to find a reason why his legs won't work.'

'Retaliation by Leviathan,' another person said.

'Yes,' the first person agreed. 'He thinks he's been smashed into the other side of next week.'

'I can't understand why God hasn't protected him,' a third person said.

I was totally baffled by all these comments. *Leviathan? Huh?* I was puzzled by the reference. I couldn't think of any Leviathan other than the one mentioned in Job. And maybe in the Psalms. But wasn't it the creature God made to frolic in the deep? The one He described in such lavish detail in the last chapters of Job? The wondrous wild beast of such terrifying majesty and august power that He doesn't want us to overlook its finer points? The one in which, as I read Scripture, He actually seemed more than pleased—*thrilled* and *exultant* were words that came to mind.

I was mystified. Were these people talking about the same creature I was thinking of or were they describing something else entirely?

Now, over subsequent years, I've since heard many others discuss Leviathan in similar ways. Slowly slowly,

I built up a picture of what most believers thought about it. Overwhelmingly and chillingly negative is probably a fair understatement.

I wasn't ever sure how accurate these perceptions were. However they were sufficiently detailed that, on the day I finally encountered the spirit of Leviathan myself, I immediately recognised it.

'Wow!' I said, sensing its rushing approach. I hasten to add at this point that I'm not a seer, so I didn't have a vision of Leviathan. I sensed an entity and I knew enough about it to immediately recognise its identity.

'Wow! One of God's great creatures! The one He made to frolic in the deep! Oh! This is so...' I paused, my smile vanishing as I remembered all the seriously unpleasant stories I'd heard over the years. My thoughts did a screeching u-turn. '...quick. How do I get out of here?'

But at the same time as I paused, desperately trying to envisage a strategic retreat, so did Leviathan. It skidded to a halt in front of me. Then it cocked its head[1] and looked me up and down, as if to say, 'Your attitude isn't what I want.'

I was too nonplussed to say anything. Leviathan gave me a final narrow-eyed stare as if to say, 'You'll keep.' Then it disappeared.

I was stunned. It was such an eerie and mysterious experience I wasn't entirely sure it was all imaginary. So of course I didn't tell anyone.

Time went by.

Several months later, two of my friends emailed me on the same day. Both spoke of backlash and retaliation. And both felt they were under savage attack by Leviathan. They asked me to pray for them and to see if I had any revelation from God. So I went straight to Him and said: 'Ok, I'm praying. But what's the right thing to pray? Why is Leviathan attacking them when it didn't bother me a few months ago? I don't understand. Can You tell me the difference between what I experienced and what they are experiencing?'

God's answer was swift in coming. 'Honour,' He said.

'Honour?' I said to God. 'What does that mean?'

'Honour means *honour*,' He said. And that was the end of the conversation.

Once again, I was seriously baffled. But I emailed both my friends and suggested they go and talk to God about honour. Later that day they got back to me. They'd each had a chat to God and He'd pointed out various family members, business associates and friends they'd dishonoured in different ways. As soon as they'd repented of their behaviour, the troublesome situations they'd been experiencing suddenly turned around.

Honour!

Could that be the answer? Was it going to be really *that* simple to overcome the spirit of Leviathan? Just be careful and intentional about honour?

Initially this strategy was an incredible success. But only initially.

I was facilitating a prayer ministry session for a woman when she suddenly jumped from her chair. 'A scorpion has just leapt onto my back.'

Unlike me, she was a seer. In the spirit realm, she'd discerned the arrival of an entity that, in the natural, would have been a scorpion.

Now, a scorpion has a stinging tail—and a stinging or lashing tail is a common symbol of Leviathan. In fact, that's one of the easiest ways to identify it: look for the tail. Now this advice might seem back-to-front, particularly since Leviathan has several heads. However my experience is that, when people see it in dreams or open visions, it's the tail that betrays it.[2] This is a general rule regardless of its appearance as a scorpion, crocodile, alligator, stingray or even a silent, silver robot trailing a long barbed stinger.[3]

When discussing Job 41:1—the beginning of an entire chapter describing the untamed and untameable nature of Leviathan—many commentaries take the view it's a crocodile. Yet no crocodile has a flame-throwing mouth or smoking nostrils (Job 41:19–21). And since the fire-breathing aspect is so like the old tales of predatory dragons, some researchers suggest Leviathan might be a survivor of the age of dinosaurs.

The woman who'd seen the scorpion leap onto her back was quite agitated. But, having learned that Leviathan's legal rights stem from dishonour, I asked, 'These men you just mentioned a moment ago—have you dishonoured them?'

'Oh, yes,' she admitted. 'Big time.'

'Well, how about you repent of that?' I said.

She agreed and, to her amazement, the scorpion disappeared. Then, just a minute later, as we returned to the issue she'd actually come to resolve, she jumped again. 'There's something even bigger coiling around me. It's huge! Like a dragon.'

Leviathan again? I was startled. *How could it possibly be back so soon?* 'Is there anyone else you've dishonoured?' I asked. 'Anyone the Lord is specifically bringing to mind at the moment?'

'Too many people to name,' she said.

Oh, this is way too big, I thought. 'Maybe we can ask God to put a hold on this dishonour matter so we can come back to it later,' I said. 'Otherwise we'll wind up with unfinished business.'

The woman frowned. 'You asked about God mentioning something specific. He's saying "cosmic entities". I don't even know what that means.'

She might not have known but I did. I'd come across the expression in the writings of Tom Hawkins.[4] 'It means angels, fallen and unfallen. Unholy and holy. Principalities, powers, world-rulers. Goddesses and godlings of other religions.'

'Like Buddha?' she asked.

I nodded. 'Exactly.'

She looked stunned. 'It's not ok to go into a Buddhist temple and curse the idol?'

It was my turn to be stunned. 'No,' I said. 'There's Scripture that warns against that.'

'There is?' She was aghast. 'But I've led teams into all sorts of temples for this purpose.'

I directed her attention to the book of Jude:

> *These people... relying on their dreams, defile the flesh, reject authority, and blaspheme the glorious ones. But when the archangel Michael, contending with the devil, was disputing about the body of Moses, he did not presume to pronounce a blasphemous judgment, but said, "The Lord rebuke you." But these people blaspheme all that they do not understand, and they are destroyed by all that they, like unreasoning animals, understand instinctively. Woe to them!*
>
> Jude 1:8–11 ESV

Read the book of Jude. It's only 25 verses in total. It will probably take you less than five minutes.

'Blaspheming the glorious ones' is another way of saying cursing and reviling, insulting and abusing, despising and ridiculing, swearing at and dishonouring these *angelic majesties*. That's what some versions call them. Others call them *great dignitaries*.

Yet, over the last few decades, many believers have been taught to declare a covering of the blood of Jesus over themselves, then take back territory by cursing demons as well as satanic powers. They've experienced retaliation so often they go into battle expecting it. Some people have even died shortly after entering shrines, temples or religious grottoes to face off with the spirit of the place. Their friends don't doubt their deaths were reprisal for the action they took against the enemy.

But their friends are also baffled that God hasn't protected these bold and fearless warriors.

But the damage is rarely due to reprisal. It simply isn't necessary. Leviathan doesn't need to exert itself in retaliation, revenge or retribution of any level. It can sit back, relax, blow a few smoke rings from its nostrils and enjoy watching them float away—while waiting for the inevitable. We're doing its work for it.

The fact is: these bold and fearless warriors defy the standing orders of their Commander-in-Chief, the Lord of Hosts, *not* to engage the enemy in this particular way. We find His clear instructions in the Book of Jude; and they are confirmed in the second epistle of Peter. In every disastrous account I've heard of people intentionally cursing a spirit, I've realised that the Holy Spirit also bears witness to these joint warnings. There's always been a moment in the story when a cautionary word was spoken or some sort of alarm rang out—but it was ignored every time.

Brian wasn't looking for trouble. But it found him.

He saw a promotional advertisement for a special ceremony celebrating the sister-city relationship between his hometown and a city in Japan. Deciding to see what it entailed, Brian arrived to see a party of Shinto priests, dancers and chanters carrying a small shrine up and down every street in the central business district. Finally they stopped in the main square where they dedicated the city and its civic administration to the *kami*—spirits and holy powers of landscape, nature beings, and deceased individuals—that are venerated in their religion. As part of this dedication rite, they warded off all evil forces and any other deities present.

Down by the river, other ritual festivities were being conducted. Priests and performers on stationary barges were chanting loudly and making copious use of incense, smoke and candles. One worshipper incessantly beat a heavy metal gong in a steady rhythm, *clang! clang! clang-clang-clang!*

A fireworks display intended especially for the attending deities lasted about fifteen minutes. There were three patterns of pyrotechnics. A star, then a ring, then something like an arrow that went through the ring. The festival coordinator announced over the public address system, 'This Ceremony is not only blessing and dedicating, but also cleansing your city and its river from the presence and control of all other gods and deities of other religions brought into this city.' Then a radio commentator added excitedly, 'Think about that, people! Aren't we so fortunate to now have our own patron deity to call upon and to look after us and to protect our future?'

Brian had seen enough. He went home and he prayed. And from that day forward, his life started to fall apart. Whenever it seemed he was just about to get back on top of things again, disaster would strike. Backlash would come out of nowhere. Brian doesn't remember what he prayed that day—and that is not unexpected. One of the closest allies of Leviathan is Ziz, the spirit of forgetting.[5] And it works at dulling your memory because, after all, that's the easiest and most efficient way to keep you a captive of hell: if you can't remember, you don't even know you need to repent, let alone what it's all about.

However, Brian knows himself well enough to admit that his prayers at the time would have been disrespectful. He would have called down curses on the priests and their actions.

Brian wasn't visiting Japan when he observed this ceremony. He was simply checking out what was going on in his hometown.

As was James.

Quite independently of Brian, he also attended a sister-city ceremony. He was with a group of people from his church who were intending to head off as missionaries to Japan in the near future, and he simply went along to soak up some culture. James found himself in the front row when a Shinto priest came along, handing out paper dolls.

Feeling awkward and uncomfortable, he moved away and went to find a rubbish bin. He was about the throw the doll in, but decided instead to tear it in half. As he did, an electric-like jolt spiked up his right arm.

Realising something was wrong he went to get prayer from his team leader—and soon felt better. It didn't occur to him there would be further repercussions. However, unknown to him, his action started the countdown on a time bomb and, after ticking away for several years, the clock finally reached zero. That happened, of course, while he was visiting Japan.

In tearing the doll in two, James had created a covenant symbol.[6] More significantly, he'd done so while the angelic principalities of at least two different nations were in attendance at this spiritually-charged event. No doubt some of the eight million *kami* alleged to exist would have been observing the festivities. In addition some of the local spirit beings would also have been keeping an eye on the scene—if nothing else to check out what the *kami* were up to while they were on a turf not their own.

James had ensured he was a marked man and, from that point on, demonic forces awaited their opportunity to tear up his life just as he'd torn up the paper doll.

It didn't happen at once. They waited sufficient time for him to forget what had happened so he wouldn't make any immediate connection back to ripping up the doll. Plus they wanted to ensure maximised destruction. That's a key element as to why we don't always see immediate retaliation: it's simply not the most opportune time for high-level havoc.

When it comes to the legal rights of cosmic powers like Leviathan, it's imperative to keep one spiritual principle in mind: *we reap what we sow*.

It doesn't matter how innocently we sow or how ignorantly either. Our actions plant spiritual 'seed' and ultimately have consequences. These happen regardless of our intentions and independent of whether we're Scripturally misinformed or not. It's a perfectly impartial, totally just spiritual law. There's a parallel in the natural world: *to every action, there is an equal and opposite reaction*.

An action that seems trivial to us may be far from insignificant in the spirit realm. It may constitute a declaration of war.

Both James and Brian acted in ignorance. But not everyone does.

So often believers defer to peer pressure rather than the witness of the Holy Spirit to their hearts. And it's not always a simple—or even advisable—thing to walk away. In a tour group entering a temple, it may be incredibly hard to make a stand without dishonouring someone or something. On arrival in New Zealand at Auckland International Airport, it's impossible to avoid the tomokanga, the carved Maori gateway symbolising a spiritual portal from darkness to light.[7] The passage under the arch is the only way in for travellers. The same is true for many roads in Japan. The torii gates are inescapable. Or what about those tricky situations—like a wedding that begins with a smoking ceremony to invoke the blessing of the spirits of the land?

Life is full of traps. But God is not fooled: He knows when we deliberately put one foot in a snare or when our transgressions are accidental. We still reap what we sow, but when we sow unintentionally, He minimises the reaping as long as possible.

Many so-called 'powerful' prayers are scattered across the internet for overthrowing Leviathan. Some of these display mockery and contempt towards various denizens of the spirit realm. Many people feel uneasy—but they go ahead and make the declarations anyway. Some people actually know the warnings in Jude and Peter but become convinced, in the pressure-cooker atmosphere of a conference, that the speaker on stage has a higher revelation than these apostles.

Consequently the retaliation is often sudden, savage, life-threatening. Don't be influenced to ignore the plain words of Scripture!

It leads to desperation for a solution: a quick fix, a *still more* powerful prayer, special insight for an appeal in the courts of heaven, appropriate wording for a declaration to cover and reverse the situation, the fervent intercession of a group of powerful prayer warriors, a finesse that works immediately—anything, in fact, to stop Leviathan in its tracks.

Now whenever I see prayers labelled 'powerful', red flags go up. I sense the possibility of a formula. There are prayers in this book but none of them are powerful. Not one. They are—on the contrary—weak, insignificant and at times totally pathetic—but they work by providing an opportunity to connect with Jesus. He is the One who empowers prayer as we unite our crumb of faith to His faith while He intercedes for us before the Father's throne. It isn't the prayer that's powerful; it's the One who mediates on our behalf.

So what do we do if we've made a terrible mistake, conformed to public pressure and used a 'powerful prayer' laced with dishonour? Actually, 'mistake' is not really the word because, when we know better, we're in open defiance of God.

The Scriptural principle behind Paul's argument in 1 Corinthians 8:1–13 about unholy covenants is twofold. First, for leaders: take care not to shepherd others into violating their conscience by exercising your freedom in Christ. Second, for followers: if you happen to have misgivings about a spiritual practice, don't be swayed by other people. If you give in and follow their example, you've committed a sin—regardless of whether an actual sin is involved or not. That's because, in ignoring the voice of your conscience, you've dishonoured the Spirit of God. This is the case, regardless of whether your conscience is correct or not. The dishonour is in placing the advice of men above the promptings of the Holy Spirit.

My suggestion in any of these circumstances is to acknowledge the betrayal and throw ourselves on God's mercy. Whenever we're seeking something resembling a formula, we need to recognise our relationship with Him is in a desperate state. The grace we need is not that of a higher level prayer, for there is no such thing. Nor is it that of a declaration to bind Leviathan and render it impotent, for Scripture tells us that isn't going to happen. The grace we need is an awareness that we've consciously wounded the Father's heart and, instead of seeking Him, we've been looking to salvage the situation through some method that worked for someone else in similar circumstances. We need the grace to *want* to connect with His aching heart and the grace to know we need to ask Jesus for help to repair the relationship. And the grace to humble ourselves enough to simply plead for mercy.

So back to the question of what we do when we're suddenly stuck in the invidious position of either having to cross an unholy threshold or else make a scene causing dishonour. Some people would make a bold stand and refuse to cross anyway. But when we honour God by dishonouring others, we simply rupture relationships. Besides, Jesus—on at least one occasion—went into a pagan shrine.[8]

So what I do is say something along the following lines:

> 'I am a covenant child of Yahweh and I am covered by His armour, overshadowed by the prayer shawl of His Son, the Lord Jesus Christ, and protected by the power of His saving blood. I mean no dishonour by entering this place. I am here simply to honour the person who invited me. Any action of mine, done in ignorance of the customs of this place, that might be construed as raising a covenant with the spirits in residence here, is absolutely and for all time null and void. If any spirit wishes to contend the legality of this statement, then that spirit should take up the matter directly with Jesus of Nazareth, my covenant defender. I ask for His kiss to armour me as I enter and I say to any enemy of my Lord in this place, "The Lord rebuke you!"'

Let me stress again this is not a formula. It's a starting point to help guide you into a heart-to-heart conversation with the Holy Spirit as to how to honour everyone, as Scripture directs us, without dishonouring God.

Prayer

I strongly recommend that all the prayers in this book are read through carefully *before* being prayed aloud with intentionality. If you feel a check in your spirit from the Holy Spirit about any aspect of the prayer, then heed it. Put off praying until you receive permission from God.

It is vitally important to recognise that prayer is about relationship with the Father. It is not intended as a formula. The prayers in this book are meant to be guidelines; they are nothing in themselves; they are not powerful or guaranteed; they are meant as a starting point, not as an end in themselves.

The shift from dishonour to honour is only possible as you hold onto the hem of Jesus' prayer shawl and ask Him to mediate before the Father for for you. In the end, it's all about Him!

Father God, even when I think I live in isolation and solitude You are with me. Though I travel to the ends of the earth I cannot escape You; nor can I escape the backlash Leviathan delivers for my sins of dishonour and disrespect. Help me, Father, to honour and respect both You and others in ways that are in tune with the heart of Jesus. Teach me how to make wise decisions and how to be vigilant and prayerful.

Abba Father, Daddy, so often I think You are just like my earthly dad who failed to protect me. However, Abba, You are not like that at all. Your protection is always over me but, when I decide to act in disrespectful and dishonourable ways, I remove myself from Your covering. I'm the one who puts myself in a place where I am outside of Your protection and covenantal defence.

When I simply reap what I have sown in terms of dishonour, remind me of the moment of sowing so I can bring it to You.

Lord, I repent of ever blaming You for situations that were all of my own creation and the result of my own decisions. Lord, grant me a spirit of discernment and wisdom. Open my eyes to Your choices.

Lord, write in the very depths of my heart that all are worthy of the dignity and respect that is afforded to royalty. Because that is what *they* are; that is what *we* are; that is what *I* am. Lord, engrave this on my heart.

Forgive me, Father, for my sins of dishonour. I ask Your grace and mercy for having wounded Your heart. I failed to seek You and instead decided to do things my way. I thought I could manage on my own. Grant me the grace, Father, to ask Jesus to help repair our relationship.

Come, Lord Jesus, I am ready and I ask Your love, protection and compassion.

I ask this in Your name. Amen.

2

Seize the Day

IN *GOD'S FOOTPRINT IN BUSINESS*, Alistair Petrie tells the story of a privately owned pharmaceutical company in dire trouble. The Christian owner asked for prayer when the business was on the brink of collapse. Their computer system had crashed and the malfunction could not be traced. After some inquiries, it transpired the problem began on the day a new computer programmer was hired. A very religious man but not of a Christian persuasion, he'd hung a raw chicken in the workspace as an offering for an auspicious beginning to his new job. When the owner repented of allowing this to happen, things started to turn around.[9]

Whenever we're transitioning into something new—whether it's a new job, a new status such as marriage, a promotion to a new position, a new business venture—we're on a threshold. Scripturally speaking, the most important personal threshold is that into our calling. Christian believers have largely forgotten the ancient understanding—embedded throughout Scripture—that all thresholds require a sacrifice. The very religious computer programmer knew the old ways. But, in following them, he legally invited another spirit into his workplace. In fact, he used the concept of threshold covenant to bring a covenant defender—who was *not* the Holy Spirit—into that space.

The owner had authority to repudiate this invitation but, until the business was on the edge of closure, he didn't exercise it.

Now it's quite probable the programmer hadn't invited in the spirit of Leviathan. Noting the constriction and wasting that resulted, it seems far more likely he was sacrificing to either the spirit of Python[10] or that of Rachab. Nevertheless, they work in consort with Leviathan to bring about situations where spiritual retaliation can be put into effect.

Jesus gave us authority over Leviathan. When the seventy disciples returned, rejoicing, from preaching and healing, He said:

> *'I saw Satan fall like lightning from heaven. Behold, I have given you authority to tread on serpents and scorpions, and over all the power of the enemy, and nothing shall hurt you.'*
>
> Luke 10:18–19 ESV

From the context, the 'scorpions' are enemy spirits—Leviathan and its kindred. And, according to Jesus, we have authority over them and nothing shall hurt us. However, the reason I've begun this book with stories of the harm inflicted by Leviathan is to show how damaging a simplistic understanding of this verse is.

Too many believers exercise authority without divine permission. Even Jesus who, by His own admission, had *all* authority didn't do that. As He was being arrested in the Garden of Gethsemane, He rebuked Peter for wielding a sword:

> *'Do you think that I cannot appeal to My Father, and He will at once put at My disposal more than twelve legions of angels?'*

Matthew 26:53 NAS

So often we come up with a 'good idea' and fail to ask the Holy Spirit whether it's a 'God idea'. Even the apostles weren't immune to persisting with a 'good idea' that wasn't a 'God idea'.

> *Paul and his companions travelled throughout the region of Phrygia and Galatia, having been kept by the Holy Spirit from preaching the word in the province of Asia. When they came to the border of Mysia, they tried to enter Bithynia, but the Spirit of Jesus would not allow them to.*

Acts 16:6–7 NIV

Now Paul had the authority to go into Asia—after all, the gospel mandate was to preach the Good News to the entire world. But the Holy Spirit and the Spirit of Jesus did not extend permission to him.

Today we're apt to think that, if we possess authority, we don't require permission. But that's the mentality of power. Not of honour. Not of love. Not of courtesy.

The Father gives us authority in Jesus—but many times we must intentionally seek His permission as well. Many believers forget spiritual authority is *deputised* divine power. God has delegated power to us so we can uphold His rule and extend His *shalom* throughout the world. But our desire for security on our own terms often leads us to neglect tempering authority with love and peace. Instead we twist it into control over others. And our twisting in turn attracts the twisting of Leviathan.

Joshua had authority to take the Promised Land. No question about it. He'd been commissioned by God Himself, told three times by Him to '*be strong and courageous*' and promised that every place he put his foot would be given to him. But we see that, even so, his assigned and delegated power didn't mean he could do whatever he liked:

> *Now it happened that while Joshua was near Jericho, he looked up and much to his amazement, he saw a man standing in front of him, holding a drawn sword in his hand! Joshua approached him and asked him, 'Are you one of us, or are you with our enemies?'*

> *'Neither,' he answered. 'I have come as commander of the Lord's Army.'*

Joshua 5:13-14 ISV

What an extraordinary response! It's a threat to the almost universal belief that Paul's question in Romans 8:31—*If God is for us, who can be against us?*—self-evidently proclaims He always has our back.

We want power—regardless of permission. We want to interpret authority as the right to trample on objections and dismiss any inconvenient restrictions. The reason so many believers today get smashed in spiritual warfare is because they ignore God's battleplan and, in the process, hand over legal rights to the enemy. Allegiance to God is tested through obedience. The commander of the Lord's Army—the actual source of Joshua's authority—wasn't necessarily *for* the Israelites. Angelic reinforcement was conditional and depended on honouring God by following His strategy.

But it's not just God we're called to honour. Peter tells us:

> *Honour everyone. Keep on loving the community of believers, fearing God, and honouring the king.*

1 Peter 2:17 ISV

Everyone. That's who we're called to honour. Are there any exceptions? Apparently not. Back when Peter was writing, the 'king' was the Roman emperor—a pagan persecutor of believers, an arch-enemy of the Christian community.

In his second epistle, Peter says it would be far better for those who '*despise authority*' and '*slander angelic majesties*' to have never known the Lord Jesus Christ. (2 Peter 2:10–20 BSB) That's an incredibly serious charge!

Some people despise authority by refusing to honour their leaders. Some leaders despise authority by exercising it without honour towards their followers. Some leaders understand honour as *complete submission* and, by that, they mean their followers must never question their decisions, or speak against their behaviour or fail to respond unconditionally to their instructions.

However, as I have indicated in the extensive discussion in *God's Panoply*, the problem with the Greek word for 'submit' is that it has no direct equivalent in Hebrew. Sure there's a word for 'submit' in Hebrew but it has entirely the opposite sense to the Greek. That's why Paul went to such lengths to explain the particular nuance he wants us to draw out of his use of it: it's because 'submit' in Greek means *to place yourself under the control of another*; while in Hebrew it's *to lift another person up*.

A power reversal results from the traditional translation 'submit' rather than the perfectly legitimate alternative 'support'. This unusual rendering[11] happens to convey the Hebrew sense behind the multi-faceted Greek word. And when we think about it, mutual support makes a lot more sense than reciprocated submission.

> *'Submit to one another out of reverence for Christ.'*
>
> Ephesians 6:21 NIV

The Contemporary English Version has a lot to recommend it at this point:

> *'Honour Christ and put others first.'*

There is no indication in Scripture that 'honouring' means never correcting our leaders, closing our eyes to their abuse or offering them the trust that should be reserved only for God. Nathan challenged David over his abuse of power; Jesus rebuked Peter—moments after commending his faith—for being the mouthpiece of the satan; Paul likewise confronted Peter over his hypocrisy.

Honouring others does not mean either speaking positively or else shutting up. That's not honouring; it's ego-stroking. Honouring means mutual encouraging, praying for, blessing, uplifting, defending, protecting, correcting, warning, clarifying, rebuking—each at the right time and in the right way. Are we going to get it wrong? Absolutely! Many times. This is why God has given us tools for reconciliation: repentance and forgiveness. Honouring includes forgiving and being forgiven, as well as repenting and experiencing others repent of their behaviour towards us.

> *'Honour your father and mother'—which is the first commandment with a promise—'so*

> *that it may go well with you and that you may enjoy long life on the earth.'*

> Ephesians 6:2–3 NIV

Honour of parents comes with a promise. Dishonour of parents forfeits the promise: it isn't going to go well with you if you've condemned them in your heart. Yet how can we honour parents when they've behaved—and even continue to behave—dishonourably? We forgive. Seventy times seven.

Now this doesn't mean we put ourselves in harm's way. Scripture clearly indicates that, when the spirit of abuse and perversity is inspiring a person's evil behaviour, we should not associate with them.

My mother often tells the story—with the full permission of the woman concerned—of a young lady so crippled by a mystery illness she had to lie on a mattress to receive prayer ministry. She was in such great pain she couldn't even sit up for any length of time. The woman refused to forgive her mother, whom she described as being 'like Hitler'. Eventually realising that unforgiveness was like a chain binding her to her mother, she grudgingly spoke out her pardon. A few minutes after she'd struggled painfully out the door, she bounded back. She was yelling, 'Look at me! Look at me!' as she glowed at my mum. 'I can walk! And you didn't even pray for healing.'

'Perhaps,' my mother said, 'when you gave God permission to take the bitterness out of your heart, He took the opportunity to take it out of your bones as well.'

It's clear we can't dishonour any*one* without consequence. We can't dishonour any*thing* either. Even something as abstract as a 'Day'.

I received an email from a woman in a tiny town on the east coast of New Zealand. The fact the town was tiny, the fact it was on the east coast and the fact it was in New Zealand were all incredibly significant but, for the best part of a year, they went right over my head. The woman asked me if I had any insight into why her life was a see-saw of violence and false accusation. She'd recover from one incident only to reel into the next. Despite her innocence, she was constantly having the blame pinned on her. One incident of retaliation had been so severe she'd suffered brain damage. And although she'd had a great deal of valuable prayer ministry and experienced many minor breakthroughs, the cause of the constant reprisals eluded her.

She'd forgiven, she'd repented, she'd renounced every vow she could think of and, as I read her story, I couldn't think of anything she might have missed. So I looked up the local legends from the town where she lived, just in case it was something to do with the 'genius loci', *the spirit of the place*. The old stories spoke of a pair of guardian taniwha in the river.

The word 'taniwha' is Māori for *monster*. It contains the element 'tan' which, probably not coincidentally, is

Hebrew for *monster*, and also happens to occur in the name 'Levia*than*'. The component 'than' at the end of the word can also be transcribed 'tan'. Certainly something like Leviathan was part of the geography of the place *but...* why attack this woman? Why the continual backlash against her in particular? It seemed to go back as far as she could remember.

It didn't make any sense. *Unless...*

Unless... it was something to do with that totally incomprehensible verse in the third chapter of Job about Leviathan.

> 'May it be cursed by those who curse the day—those prepared to rouse Leviathan.'

Job 3:8 BSB

In this passage, Job was talking about the day he was born. *But how, I wondered, was it possible for anyone to curse something as intangible as a 'day'? How on earth could anyone, no matter how skilled they were at activating malice, actually seize a 'day' and dishonour it?*

I had absolutely no idea.

But I didn't let ignorance stop me. I asked this woman, 'Is it possible that someone cursed the day you were born?'

Immediately she related the story of a tragedy that occurred in the family home on the day of her birth. Some superstitious members of her family blamed her—even as a new-born baby, even though she was not actually present at the time—for the disaster.

I have subsequently come across several other people in similar circumstances. In fact, mention 'brain damage' and 'retaliation' in the same conversation to me, and I now ask as a matter of routine: 'Is it possible someone cursed the day you were born?'

Because cursing the day someone was born rouses Leviathan.[12]

I don't know what a 'Day' looks like to God, but I do know this: it is not abstract or inanimate. I don't know whether it's a 'creature' in God's eyes—a spirit entity of some ineffable, transcendent kind—but I suspect it's akin to the *angelic majesties* mentioned by Jude and Peter. It's definitely something that can be dishonoured. And demeaning it brings forth, in the fullness of time, a whirlwind of retaliation that increases in force as the years go by.

Innocence is not relevant once Leviathan is roused. It's immaterial. Leviathan smells dishonour on us and it moves against that dishonour with extraordinary zeal.

Sometimes the dishonour it detects is the contempt we've directed at others.

Sometimes the dishonour is like a defiling blanket that's been wrapped around us by others—while they've poured out the contents of a bottle of toxic shame. We've come to own that corroded blanket and agree with the lies embedded in it. Deep in our hearts, we've learned to be complicit with it all. We believe that we deserve the defamation and disrespect meted out to us.

Sometimes the dishonour is about reviling spiritual beings, sacred things or hallowed spaces—regardless of whether these are holy or fallen.

Sometimes the dishonour is about trying to use the blood of Jesus to nullify the Word of God.

Sometimes the dishonour is about trying to leverage God's grace to avoid the natural repercussions from our defiance of Him.

Sometimes it's about flouting God's will. And sometimes it's about spitting in God's face. He's apparently ok with anger; but not with contempt, ridicule or derision—at Himself or any aspect of His creation. We dishonour Him when we dishonour His creation, even His fallen creation, whether it's humanity or a spiritual entity.

It's worth repeating something I wrote not long back: God is not fooled; He knows when we deliberately put one foot in a snare or when our transgressions are accidental. He knows when a mistake is due to ignorance or when it's outright treason against the Kingdom of God.

As we noted before: we still reap what we sow, but when we sow unintentionally, He minimises the reaping for as long as possible. He shields us from harm—up to a point.

But not forever.

When I first realised how significant honour was, I naturally went looking for a mention of it in connection with Leviathan. But I couldn't find anything. It took me quite a while to shift my thinking around sufficiently to realise that it *is* there—just not in the way I'd expected. At the end of the Book of Job, God extols the peerless nature of Leviathan, saying that nothing on earth is its equal. Then He adds:

> *He looks on everything that is high; He is king over all the sons of pride.*
>
> Job 41:34 NAS

> *He looks down on all the haughty; he is king over all the proud.*
>
> Job 41:34 BSB

Arrogant people naturally dishonour others—often in ways they'd be outraged to receive in return. The Greeks taught that the goddess Nemesis follows after hubris—that is, an inescapable avenger hunts down the haughty and the proud. It's simply another way of saying: 'Pride goes before a fall.' Nemesis—at least in terms of functional qualities—is not unlike Leviathan.

Now, in fact, by saying Leviathan is '*king of the sons of pride*', God tells us that pride is a sign of loyalty to Leviathan. And Leviathan is not a gentle king.

Scripture tells us that honour is a consequence of being humble:

> *Pride ends in humiliation, while humility brings honour.*
>
> Proverbs 29:23 NLT

Family pride and ethnic pride are, in my experience, two major triggers for a fortress of denial to activate itself. But there's one kind of pride I've noticed that is rarely, if ever, exposed. I've seen prayers for breaking the power of Leviathan that involve renouncing pride of all kinds—including in a state, city or sporting team. But I've never seen one renouncing patriotic pride in our own nation.

I'm old enough to remember the days before Australians had any substantial pride in their country. I also recall the moment when the seismic change occurred. It was September 1983. After a stay of 132 years as the prestigious ward of the New York Yacht Club, the America's Cup was finally won by a foreign challenger—Australia.

In the spiritual world, however, I'm convinced it wasn't so much that the Australian team won, as the American defenders lost. I believe seven words spoken by Dennis Conner—a Christian—and the skipper of the defending yacht, *Liberty*, sealed victory for his opponents. 'We cannot lose,' he told waiting reporters. 'God is an American.'

When patriotism slides into blasphemy, God is dishonoured and Leviathan has a free hand. In an unprecedented defeat, *Liberty* lost the next three races, allowing *Australia II* to come from behind to take the prize from the United States for the first time in history.

Patriotism requires constant vigilance so that it does not become an idol. 'My country—right or wrong!'[13] speaks of national fervour, bordering on blind worship, which rightly needs the stern corrective of 'My country, right or wrong; if right, to be kept right; and if wrong, to be set right.'[14]

One of the most famous symbols of Chinese culture is the dragon. It also features strongly in Japanese, Korean and Vietnamese stories. It's no coincidence that nations in which a high value is placed on honour are associated with dragon festivals—after all, the dragon Leviathan rules over the sons of pride and watches out for dishonour.

For many Asian people the most difficult issue connected with prayer ministry is recognising that, contrary to their own deeply held belief that they've always honoured their parents, they are actually no different from the rest of the world. Coming into the self-awareness that they've mentally condemned their parents' behaviour is so counter-cultural it's comparatively rare. This is particularly true when parents have self-sacrificed to give the children every opportunity, but have not given them the gift of their own time.

That's why Leviathan has such a deep hold there. But at least it's out in the open in these countries. Unlike many other nations.

'Not even God Himself could sink this ship.'

So said an employee of the White Star Line at the launch of the *Titanic*, 31 May 1911. Although, strictly speaking, the word 'unsinkable' was never used to advertise the ship, it was bandied about by the ship-builders and the owners. The ill-fated ship was considered indestructible and the colossal confidence placed in it was, in part, a source of its own downfall. Six messages were received from other ships near to the *Titanic*'s route, warning of 'bergs, growlers and sea ice'. But the ship did not reduce its speed—it rushed recklessly on into its infamous fatal collision.

We don't need a degree in rocket science to see the cause-effect link between pride and a fall, or even dishonour and retaliation.

Pride was also a primary factor in the collision between the *SS Admiral Nakhimov* and the bulk carrier *Pytor Vasev* in the Black Sea on 31 August 1986. The carrier had a cargo of oats and barley, and the cruise liner had 888 passengers along with 346 crew. 423 of those onboard died when the cruiser sank. Both captains were eventually found guilty of criminal negligence.

They were both aware the other ship was on a collision course but, too proud to yield, they left it until too late to change direction.

So even if you didn't know of the existence of Leviathan, you should still be able to observe the dynamic of pride-preceding-a-fall operating in everyday life. *Liberty,* the *Titanic* and the *SS Admiral Nakhimov* aside, we've all seen that, sooner or later, payback in inevitable in situations of dishonour. Bullying, harassment and abuse can go on for a long time but sooner or later the tables are turned. Even if the spiritual law of sowing and reaping didn't exist for balance to be restored, our human need for justice means we want to see the perpetrator receive back in kind what they've meted out to us.

Now the higher forms of dishonour are obvious: contempt, ridicule, insults, cheating, shunning, trolling, doxing, flame wars, incitement to suicide. But what about the lesser forms? Rarely or never being on time or replying to emails, returning phone calls, remembering a person's name, acknowledging a gift, giving a definite answer to an invitation, registering before turning up at an event, saying thank you, keeping a confidence, apologising for a mistake.

Small honours used to be called 'common courtesy'. But they've become very uncommon.

Let me hasten to say that honour does *not* mean agreeing unilaterally with others. If you agree with every word your pastor says, you've made him the mouthpiece of God—and dishonoured the Holy Spirit. Being 'anointed and appointed' is no guarantee of faithfulness—after all, the anointed cherub who fell from Eden became the satan.

Disagreement is not hatred, dishonour or discourtesy—it's the rightful exercise of our freedom of intellect. Mature believers can disagree with civility and, in these circumstances, if anyone takes offence at another's deeply held conviction, then they're revealing their own insecurity.

And my insecurity does not mean you've actually dishonoured me. On the other hand, it doesn't mean that you haven't, either.

Nor does Leviathan have to be behind every act of retaliation that we suffer. Sometimes we simply bring disaster on ourselves. Yet Leviathan can take tiny opportunities to ignite a spark that brings down a rain of wildfire on all involved.

Honour everyone.

Honour God most of all.

They seem such simple instructions. Yet Scripture is full of stories about people who honoured others more than God. There was Solomon who honoured his wives more than God. There was Eli who honoured his sons more than God. There was Balaam who honoured his employer more than God. There was Absalom who honoured his advisors more than God. There was Gideon who almost honoured his parents more than God—and Jesus who warned about it. There was Peter who honoured the men sent by James more than God. There was Hezekiah who honoured his position more than God.

Being honoured more than God sets us up for deadly addiction. We need constant affirmation of our status; we consider ourselves beyond reproach, above correction and outside rebuke; we see other points of view as a threat or as disrespect; we retreat to an echo chamber where we expect our highest qualities to be repeatedly confirmed to us; we place the blame for our mistakes on others and we collect information on them to ensure we stay on top. In short, we become narcissistic.

Unless we allow God to bring us down off the pedestal, then sooner or later, Leviathan will.

Prayer

A reminder: read the prayer through carefully *before* saying aloud with intentionality. If you feel a check in your spirit from the Holy Spirit about any aspect of it, then heed the prompt. Put off praying until you receive permission from God.

Father God, I am sometimes so confused, so twisted in my thinking, so one-sided in wanting to receive honour but not to give it freely, I realise I hardly know You as the one who always honours us. You are courteous towards us, Abba; You never manipulate us to choose Your will. You do not control our minds or our hearts, even when we surrender to You. Instead You allow us freedom to align ourselves with You or to go our own way.

Father God, thank You for the law of sowing and reaping. Thank You that it is an essential part of Your divine justice and that it is meant to bring natural blessing into our lives. Lord, forgive me for wanting to bend it back on itself and coil it around so that I don't have to put up with the consequences of my own actions. Forgive me for secretly wanting a twister like Leviathan in my life for my own convenience, so that I don't receive payback for my own sins. Forgive me for my arrogance in treating others in a way I wouldn't want to be treated myself.

I repent, Lord. I am sorry. A lot of the time I'm sorry for myself more than I'm sorry for those I've hurt. So I ask Jesus of Nazareth to come as my mediator to empower my words of repentance. And I ask the Holy Spirit to come as my counsellor to give me a sense of how much my dishonour has affected others.

Father, I so often think I honour You in what I think, do and say but I often create an idol of my own intentions. I excuse myself when my actions don't match my intentions. I repent of falling short. Forgive me for my dishonour, Abba.

So often I say 'Jesus—only Jesus' but my words, thoughts and actions are very far from the heart and Spirit of Jesus. I repent of my conceit and self-importance. Forgive me, Father.

Sometimes I think I am humble and then I become proud of that humility. I repent of my pride and hypocrisy. Forgive me, Abba.

Father God, I forget quite often that every word I say, every action I take, even every thought I have becomes a signpost to You. Abba, forgive me for my neglect.

Father, forgive me for the times I've thought myself worthy of Your love and forgive me for the times I've thought myself not worthy of Your love. I am part of a people redeemed. Jesus alone makes us worthy. Thank You, Jesus, for all You have done for us. Thank You for standing before the Father with us and presenting us to Your Father and ours as pure and undefiled.

Jesus, show me what honour means and how to apply it in each and every circumstance of life. Show me when to uplift, or to challenge.

In Your Name
Amen

3

Heavenly Courtier

MY DAD USED TO TELL A STORY about my mum and himself. She'd say the problem with their relationship is that he lived on a pedestal. He'd retort that the real problem was she lived in a cellar. She'd counter with: 'Every time I get out of my cellar and try to connect with you, I can't reach past the base of your pedestal.'

My dad went to the USA at one point to receive some intensive training in prayer ministry. While he was there, he found people agreed with my mum about where he lived.

Taken aback, he gave considerable thought to the problem. On his return, he said to my mum: 'I've realised this pedestal is too high to get down off easily, so I've got an idea. I'm going to invite Jesus to come onto the pedestal with me. Maybe he'll bring a spiritual ladder or build a miraculous stairway.'

My mum decided to go along with this, so in their quiet time one morning, that's what they prayed. Jesus, according to my dad, almost immediately appeared on the pedestal. He took my dad's hand and jumped.

It was so unexpected, it was almost alarming.

But then—nothing. No sense of falling, no sense of tumbling, no sense of hitting the ground—in fact, no sense of anything.

The evening of the following day, some thirty-six hours later, my dad turned to my mum. 'We've landed!' he announced.

'What?' she asked, baffled. 'What are you talking about?'

'Jesus and me,' he said. 'We've just landed.' Dad looked sheepish. 'I didn't know the pedestal was *that* high.'

In the last year of his life, my dad realised he'd been programmed—even before he was born—to be the one who would restore the family honour. As part of this, and in order to please his mother, he'd followed her father's dream to become an engineer. But the problem with restoring the family honour is that you have to be *seen* doing it, so you need to build a pedestal and keep pumping it higher.

It will probably come as a surprise to absolutely no one that, in our family, honour was the highest virtue. But it was also an unspoken assumption; it was so much part of the warp and woof of family expectation that no one ever talked about it. It was just an insistent background to life.

But one day God drew my attention to it via some mysterious symbols in my own fiction that were all about the North Pole. But the North Pole in the strangest possible way: merry-go-rounds, ash trees, enormous spikes, animal tails, lamp-posts, honey, stationary stars. Who'd have thought they were all related as mythic symbols? Now whenever I find instinctive ideas outside of my conscious knowledge, I interrogate my own writing to see what God is telling me.

'What on earth,' I asked Him, 'is a Tyrian cynosure? Because that's what I've got here. It's more than the North Pole, it's a cynosure.'

'A cynosure is exactly what the dictionary says: a guiding light,' He replied. 'And Tyrian refers to honour, integrity and fidelity.'

'Well, that makes sense. Those are the things I value most in life. Those are the things I sacrifice for.'

'Yes, indeed you do.'

'Why is the North Pole like a Tyrian cynosure?'

'There are two North Poles: geographic and magnetic,' He pointed out. 'If you start out for the geographic North using a compass, it will be a considerable time before your direction starts to be seriously amiss.'

'You're telling me I'm off-track with You? I'm telling myself through what I've written that I'm off-track with You? How?'

'Honour, integrity and fidelity are part of My character. They are not Me. It is a very subtle error to worship aspects of My character, and to separate them from Me.'

When God then asked me if I'd be willing to give up honour, my instinctive response was: 'I'd rather die!'

In that instant, I knew honour was my idol. I'd taken an aspect of God's nature and elevated it above Him. Jesus was willing to humble Himself and suffer every form of humiliation and dishonour. Much as we are commanded to honour everyone, *we're not to enthrone it*. My life was full of fleshly forms of honour that I had to take to the cross and crucify. That was immensely hard. But virtues as they were, they'd become sin. They'd become more important to me than God Himself.

This is not to say I don't value the giving and receiving of honour—in fact, I do so enormously. But now, when issues of honour and dishonour come up, I take them to God and ask Him whether this is a time for humility on my part or for challenging others about their behaviour. Every situation is different. And the utmost care is required to always honour others, even while calling them to account.

A Tyrian cynosure is like Nechushtan, the bronze serpent that Moses lifted up in the wilderness at God's command to bring healing to the people. It was a good thing, indeed a 'God thing' because He'd directed its installation. Yet, centuries later, Hezekiah had to take it from the Temple and destroy it because it had become an idol.

I have characterised Leviathan in the title of this book as a spirit of retaliation but that's only one aspect of its nature. And a very limited one at that. We've already seen that it has a major concern with honour and humility and thus, conversely, with dishonour and pride.

Threshold spirits are wondrously complex entities, yet there's a tendency amongst believers who practise spiritual warfare to reduce them to a single simple function. We could characterise Python as a constrictor, Ziz as a raptor and Leviathan as a burner. Yet Python is not only a spirit of constriction but also of silence and ambiguity, divination, intimidation, seduction, illness and torment, jealousy and the demand for sacrifice. Ziz is not only a spirit of forgetting but also of falsehoods and wrongful accusation, manipulation, theft of inheritance, sexual immorality, mockery and witchcraft.[15]

Leviathan also has a multi-pronged agenda, but it rarely needs to move beyond its most elementary strategy. Most of us are quickly subject to reprisal for dishonour and because we don't repent, the backlash doesn't abate. The sting of retaliation keeps on rising, the flames of reprisal burn higher and higher.

Leviathan is only mentioned by name six times in Scripture. But that doesn't mean those are its only appearances. The six explicit references are:

(1) and (2)
> *In that day, the Lord will punish with His sword—His fierce, great and powerful sword—**Leviathan** the gliding serpent, **Leviathan** the coiling serpent; He will slay the monster of the sea.*
>
> Isaiah 27:1 NIV

(3)

> *You broke the heads of **Leviathan** in pieces, and gave him as food to the people inhabiting the wilderness.*
>
> Psalm 74:14 NKJV

I've chosen the New King James version here because it is one of the very few translations that tells us Leviathan was food for *people*, rather than *creatures*. As Arthur Burk points out,[16] the Hebrew word for *people* is 'am' and it occurs well over a thousand times in Scripture, but in this and *only* this instance, do the translators suddenly opt for *creatures*. It's clear that eating monsters is a theological bridge too far for most modern scholars, so they've made a subtle change to tone the verse back and bring it into line with our century's sensibilities.

However, in doing so, they've obscured a very significant clue about Leviathan's nature that we'll look at shortly.

(4)
> *There, the ships pass through;* **Leviathan**,
> *which you created, frolics in it.*
>
> Psalm 104:26 ISV

(5)
> *Let those who curse the day (those who
> know how to wake up* **Leviathan***) curse
> that night.*
>
> Job 3:8 GWT

> *Let them curse it that curse the day, who
> are ready to raise up their mourning.*
>
> Job 3:8 AKJV

The American King James Version takes the view that Leviathan is not a proper name in this instance but is an expression of grief and simply means *mourning*. While I agree that there will be plenty of sorrow and mourning because someone chooses to curse a day, I also think this particular translation obscures the action of Leviathan as an agent of chaos in many people's lives, starting from the day they were born.

(6)
> *'Can you pull in* **Leviathan** *with a fishhook
> or tie down its tongue with a rope?'*
>
> Job 41:1 NIV

That's it—here we have the sum total of all the verses that mention Leviathan by name in the original text. Now there are quite a few translations that bring it up more often but that's for our reading ease in English. Most of these insertions occur in the book of Job to clarify its presence throughout chapter 41. So although it is never mentioned again in the Hebrew text, you can see from the italicised words in the following just where the translators have introduced it.

> 'Can you pull in Leviathan with a hook
> or tie down his tongue with a rope?
> Can you put a cord through his nose
> or pierce his jaw with a hook?
> Will he beg you for mercy
> or speak to you softly?
> Will he make a covenant with you
> to take him as a slave for life?
> Can you pet him like a bird
> or put him on a leash for your maidens?
> Will traders barter for him
> or divide him among the merchants?
> Can you fill his hide with harpoons
> or his head with fishing spears?
> If you lay a hand on him,
> you will remember the battle and never repeat it!
> Surely hope of overcoming him is false.
> Is not the sight of him overwhelming?
> No one is so fierce as to rouse *Leviathan*.
> Then who is able to stand against Me?
> Who has given to Me that I should repay him?

Everything under heaven is Mine.
I cannot keep silent about his limbs,
his power and graceful form.
Who can strip off his outer coat?
Who can approach him with a bridle?
Who can open his jaws,
ringed by his fearsome teeth?
His rows of scales are his pride,
tightly sealed together.
One scale is so near to another
that no air can pass between them.
They are joined to one another;
they clasp and cannot be separated.
His snorting flashes with light,
and his eyes are like the rays of dawn.
Firebrands stream from his mouth;
fiery sparks shoot forth!
Smoke billows from his nostrils
as from a boiling pot over burning reeds.
His breath sets coals ablaze,
and flames pour from his mouth.
Strength resides in his neck,
and dismay leaps before him.
The folds of his flesh are tightly joined;
they are firm and immovable.
His chest is as hard as a rock,
as hard as a lower millstone!
When *Leviathan* rises up, the mighty are terrified;
they withdraw before his thrashing.
The sword that reaches him has no effect,
nor does the spear or dart or arrow.

> He regards iron as straw
> and bronze as rotten wood.
> No arrow can make him flee;
> slingstones become like chaff to him.
> A club is regarded as straw,
> and he laughs at the sound of the lance.
> His undersides are jagged potsherds,
> spreading out the mud like a threshing sledge.
> He makes the depths seethe like a cauldron;
> he makes the sea like a jar of ointment.
> He leaves a glistening wake behind him;
> one would think the deep had white hair!
> Nothing on earth is his equal—
> a creature devoid of fear!
> He looks down on all the haughty;
> he is king over all the proud.'

Job 41:1–34 BSB

This is an extremely interesting passage since it not only reveals what Leviathan is like, it also reveals God's knowledge of humanity's desire in relation to it. God wouldn't ask the questions about a pet on a leash or raising a covenant or bartering it in trade, if people didn't actually want that. He is exposing a deep-seated ambition to exert power over the most powerful.

The futility of this is pointed out in God's statement: *'If you lay a hand on him, you will remember the battle and never repeat it!'*

Some people want to bind Leviathan. The way I interpret this verse is that you could try to bind Leviathan, either physically or legally, but it wouldn't be wise. If you somehow manage it once, it won't happen again. You'll get so battered during the combat that you'll never attempt it a second time. In fact, this is the experience of all those people I mentioned at the beginning of the first chapter—they were so seriously and savagely wounded in the conflict that they simply weren't able to go up against Leviathan again. More than that, they didn't want to: they'd realised the price was too high.

'Surely hope of overcoming him is false,' says verse 9. *'Is not the sight of him overwhelming?'* You simply won't defeat Leviathan in a straight contest. God couldn't be clearer about the outcome of a conflict with this fabulous creature. Yet people constantly try to take it on in battle because Jesus gave us the authority to *'tread on serpents and scorpions, and over all the power of the enemy'* (Luke 10:19 ESV) and promised us that nothing will hurt us. As I've already pointed out, far too many believers equate authority with permission. But that is not always the case.

Verse 10 goes on to say: *'No one is so fierce as to rouse him.'* Now that particular comment is a bit perplexing considering that Job had previously mentioned those who could rouse Leviathan by cursing days. *'Let those curse it who curse the day, who are ready to rouse up Leviathan.'* (Job 3:8 ESV) As we saw in the first chapter, there are people even in today's world who have suffered from unrelenting attacks by Leviathan because the day of their birth was cursed.[17]

I think the apparent contradiction between these verses can be resolved by noting that a different context exists in these two cases. In Job 41:10, God is talking about rousing Leviathan via physical means for the purpose of killing it; while in Job 3:8, the emphasis is on rousing it via occult channeling for the purpose of using its power against others.

Each of the threshold guardians seems to have a specific occult specialty. It is very difficult to be sure, of course, what particular slant was given to ancient Hebrew words that referred to magic and whether these words were broad generalisations or precise technical terms. So treat my following comments with due caution.

The occult activity that is Leviathan's specialty is enchantment. Bearing in mind the comment I just made about the difficulty of being sure what this entails, I nevertheless believe it is different from the magical expertise of the other threshold guardians. Python[18] clearly specialises in divination. Ziz[19] apparently specialises in sorcery; Azazel[20] probably in spell-binding; and Belial[21] in mind control over crowds.

So how is enchantment different from these, and what is it? Again, I offer a strong caution about my interpretation but, taking into account tradition and folklore—which often preserves ancient memories of spiritual realities—my view is that 'enchantment' is a kind of hypnosis. It's akin to mesmerism; like that old-fashioned description of fairies who deceived humans using 'glamour' to disguise the true nature of themselves and their surroundings. And, while *glamour* now of course describes a person of alluring beauty, it was originally associated with an ability to *charm*, *bewitch* or *enchant*.

Leviathan is a creature of spectacular power and beauty. God testifies to this when He speaks of its graceful limbs and impressive form. But when we engage with it, rather than direct our attention constantly to God, we can fall prey to the glamour and the enchantment. It is a gorgeous creature of light—as God says, '*His snorting flashes with light, and his eyes are like the rays of dawn. Firebrands stream from his mouth; fiery sparks shoot forth!*' But its heart is dark and hard. Although the translation of verse 24, as shown above, says that Leviathan's chest is as hard as a rock, a more accurate rendition of the Hebrew would say that its *heart is like stone*.

The sheer loveliness of Leviathan tempts people to listen to it and covenant with it. Sometimes this will be a new covenant and sometimes it will be a re-affirmation of an ancestral covenant. God asked Job the question in verse 4: '*Will he make a covenant with you to take him as a slave for life?*' This is not necessarily a rhetorical question with a simple negative answer. Rather I believe the answer is: 'Yes and no. Sure, he'll make a covenant but not so he'll be your slave. Rather, it's so you'll be his slave.'

Many people see the majestic finale of the book of Job where God's voice emanates from a whirlwind as a divine putdown. They see God firmly and sternly reprimanding Job and reminding him of his rightful place in the universe: 'You are a creature, not the Creator. How dare you demand answers of Me! *Answers*! I'll give you *questions*!'

Now I think this interpretation is a result of cultural expectation. Job has questioned God all the way through the book. And, in fact, he's mentioned many of the very things that God questions him about: the star cluster of the Pleiades, the constellation of Orion, the ostrich, the earth suspended over the void, the gates of death, the birthing of ice. So, in my view, behind God's questions is the implication: 'I heard you, Job. I was paying attention. I was listening all the time.'

God treats Job with the deep respect of a great rabbi towards a favourite student. He returns question for question, adding a bit more information into His questions so the student can learn to follow the rabbi more closely. In Middle Eastern culture, unlike our own, a question for a question is not a sign of belittlement but rather of high honour.

That's why we need to look so carefully at the clues within God's questions about Leviathan. Because, ultimately, they contain the answers to Job's ultimate question: 'Why did I suffer like this?' And the deep answer is: 'You were facing off with Leviathan.'

And no one comes out of that encounter unscathed. Not even Jesus.

Leviathan is often imaged in Scripture as a serpent or a dragon.

> *'In that day the Lord will take His sharp, great, and mighty sword, and bring judgment on Leviathan, the fleeing serpent—Leviathan, the coiling serpent—and He will slay the dragon of the sea.'*
>
> Isaiah 27:1 BSB

This last part of this verse indicates it is a primeval water monster. So does its name. The last syllable, which can be spelled as either 'than' or 'tan', means either *monster of the deep* or *jackal*.

I don't know of anyone who has seen Leviathan in a vision or a dream as a jackal, so I'm not going to address it in this book. However I will leave it for a companion volume.[22]

The 'water monster' aspect has led translators of Job 40:25 to equate Leviathan with the Nile crocodile.[23] However, since Psalm 104:25 mentions Leviathan frolicking alongside ships on the sea, the crocodile doesn't quite ring true across the board as an image, so they've preferred to regard it in that instance as a whale.

Still these identifications seem quite wide of the mark once we factor in the flame-throwing mouth of Job 41:19.

Much as many commentators want to find a 'natural' explanation for Leviathan rather than a 'mythical' one, it's unfortunate for them that the best description really is a *dragon*.

Now as I've mentioned, people who dream about Leviathan generally see a culturally appropriate symbol with a lashing, stinging tail. On the other hand, seers who have encountered Leviathan usually report that it has seven heads. Scripture does not directly back up this depiction. However Psalm 74:14 mentions '*heads*' in the plural and I believe there are sufficient other clues scattered in various places to say that seven heads is the right number rather than, for example, six as is depicted in Greek mythology by the serpentine Hydra.[24]

Before we look more closely at the original nature of Leviathan, let me note some unusual depictions of it. Some commentators have, on the basis of Job 3:8—the verse about cursing the day—called it an eclipse-producing dragon. Others have seen it as being figurative of Egypt as an engulfing nation,[25] while Jewish folklore has equated it to the river Nile itself with its seven divisions.[26] This manages to keep the symbol of Egypt intact but perhaps it's actually meant to direct our attention towards the heavenly river that was considered to mirror and reflect the earthly Nile below. This identification may have been influenced by the connection of Leviathan's counterpart in Canaanite religion—the seven-headed Lotan—with the Litani River of Lebanon.

In Sumerian religion, a Seven-headed Serpent was slain by Ninurta,[27] who hung its body on the shining crossbeam of his chariot; and at Angkor Wat, in Cambodia, the well-restored statue of the naga shows it as a seven-headed dragonish serpent.

The connection of dragons with rivers is not confined to Egypt and Lebanon. Both the Yangtze and Yellow Rivers of China are considered to be the transformed bodies of a green and a yellow dragon who saved the world from a drought and a horde of monsters and who taught people magic spells to banish anger and pain.[28] A traditional belief—one particularly associated with the Chinese New Year—says a fish able to leap the Dragon Gate of the Yellow River will metamorphose into a dragon.

In Australia, many Dreaming stories speak of the Rainbow Serpent, normally associated with a local waterhole, waterfall or sacred pool. Each of the peoples scattered across the continent have their own tale of its interaction with their indigenous ancestors but the oldest legends tell of it emerging from the sea in the far north. This suggests that, like those creatures designated in Hebrew as 'tan' or 'than', it was originally a chaos monster that revelled in the waters of the deep.

In New Zealand, amongst the Māori people, stories of taniwha abound. These monsters generally live in pools or streams and are often considered to be the guardians of specific reaches of particular rivers. I regard it as far from coincidental that 'taniwha',[29] the general word for *monster* in the Māori language, contains 'tan', the Hebrew syllable for *monster of the deep*.[30]

I mention all these geographical associations because I want to foreshadow Leviathan's link with certain landscapes. And while such a link is not explicitly mentioned in Scripture, I believe it is coded into the story of Elijah in a very subtle way.

But before being able to demonstrate that, first we need to be able to classify Leviathan. And that's not as simple as relegating it to the ranks of the sea monsters—those creatures God created on the fifth day. I've picked the New American Standard Version here because most translations shy away from mentioning the monsters:

> *God created the great sea monsters and every living creature that moves, with which the waters swarmed after their kind, and every winged bird after its kind; and God saw that it was good.*
>
> Genesis 1:21 NAS

The word, *monsters*, is accurate since it comes from 'tan' (or 'than'), the same syllable that occurs at the end of Levia<u>than</u>. Obviously those monsters were good, at least to start with, because God saw that '*it was good*'.

Now I personally believe that, while we can class the spirit of Leviathan as a cosmic power which, in the heavenly realms, is equivalent to a sea monster in the natural world, it also belongs to the angelic class known as the seraphim. If we go back once more to examine Isaiah 27:1—'*In that day the Lord will take His sharp, great, and mighty sword, and bring judgment on Leviathan, the fleeing* **serpent**—*Leviathan, the coiling* **serpent**—*and He will slay the dragon of the sea*'—the twice-repeated word for serpent which is emphasised in bold type is 'nahas' or 'nachash'.

This is just one of several Hebrew words for *serpent*. Others include:

- 'pethen' (*serpent*, probably the *cobra*, but the word from which we derive *python*)

- 'saraph' (*serpent that is like one of the seraphim*; that is, burning and having wings—perhaps a hooded *cobra* from the 'wings' around its head and its burning venom)

- 'shephiphon' (*serpent*, perhaps a horned viper)

- 'tsepha' or 'tsiphoni' (*serpent*, probably the *viper* or *adder*)

- 'zocheleth' (*serpent* or *crawling thing*)

- 'tan' or 'tannin' (*serpent*, *dragon*, *sea monster* or *jackal*)

The use of 'nachash' to describe Leviathan tells us that it is the same kind of being, if not the very same being, as the serpent in the Garden of Eden. Some commentators think that the fact 'nachash' is used in both instances is enough to finger Leviathan as the satan. I'm not so sure. As I've looked at these different words for *serpent*, I'm aware they are not distinct categories.

Leviathan can be described as both 'tan' and 'nachash'. Python, since it also contains the syllable 'tan' at the end of its name, shares a lot in common with Leviathan. And to complicate matters, 'seraph-like' is used to describe the serpents of Numbers 21:6 which attacked the people of Israel because of their grumbling and dishonour of God—'*Then the Lord sent venomous snakes among them; they bit the people and many Israelites died.*' In the original Hebrew, *venomous snakes* is really 'nachash like seraphim'; that is, like the fiery six-winged angelic throne guardians[31] mentioned in Isaiah's vision of the divine council and the royal court of God.

In this story from the book of Numbers, God provided a remedy for the fatal bite of the serpents. He told Moses to make a bronze snake and put it on a pole so that anyone who looked upon it would live. From a combination of *bronze*, 'nechosheth', and *serpent*, 'nachash', this snake-draped staff acquired the name Nechushtan—which, as you've probably already noticed, contains the element 'tan' for a *dragon* or *sea monster*.

Curiously the word 'nechosheth', besides meaning *bronze*, also means *lust*, *harlotry* or *idolatry*. A millennium and a half after Moses lifted up the bronze serpent, Hezekiah broke Nechushtan into pieces because it had become an idol and people were burning incense to it. The words of Psalm 74:14—*You broke the heads of Leviathan in pieces*—are re-affirmed in Hezekiah's action.

Whenever we turn good into god, we re-enact the choice of Eden.

Now 'nachash' turns up in several other significant places.

- It is the type of serpent that Moses' staff turned into at the burning bush.

- It is used prophetically of the treachery of the tribe of Dan, but so is 'shephiphon'.

- It is the name of an Ammonite king.

- Most significantly, it is a word for *hissing an enchantment* or *whispering a magic spell*.

This is why I stated Leviathan's occult specialty is *enchantment*. And ultimately that particular ability is what I think distinguishes any serpent categorised as a 'nachash': whatever other features it has, it has the ability to enchant, mesmerise, hypnotise and cast a glamour. It can even convince us that beauty is not only truth, but also another way to our heavenly Father.

Because a seraph is a nachash and because Leviathan is also a nachash, I believe that Leviathan is a seraph.

I recognise that the logic is a bit dubious—but, at the present time, I'm sticking with it.[32] And as we look more closely at the little we know about the seraphim, we'll start to see a jigsaw of connections that I think fill in the gaps in the problematic logic.

> *In the year that King Uzziah died, I saw the Lord, high and exalted, seated on a throne; and the train of His robe filled the temple. Above Him were seraphim, each with six wings... And they were calling to one another: 'Holy, holy, holy is the Lord Almighty; the whole earth is full of His glory.' ...*
>
> *'Woe to me!' I cried. 'I am ruined! For I am a man of unclean lips, and I live among a people of unclean lips, and my eyes have seen the King, the Lord Almighty.'*
>
> *Then one of the seraphim flew to me with a live coal in his hand... With it he touched my mouth and said, 'See, this has touched your lips; your guilt is taken away and your sin atoned for.'*
>
> Isaiah 6:1–7 NIV

Seraphim are mentioned seven times in Scripture: four times in Isaiah, twice in Numbers and once in Deuteronomy. The references in Numbers and Deuteronomy refer to the incident where people started dying because they grumbled.

Basically this is the same scenario as we've seen in all the modern stories I related in the first chapter: retaliation for dishonouring God.

In fact, the unclean lips of Isaiah and the people complaining in the wilderness simply suggest defilement and dishonour. And it seems to me that the job of a seraph—or at least one part of this angelic office—is to ensure honour is maintained in the heavenly court. Obviously that can be done with a purifying coal or it can be done by simply removing the person.

So, if Leviathan is a seraph, then it follows he held a privileged office that required him to uphold honour within the heavenly courts and rectify anything detracting from God's glory. And perhaps the words 'the year that King Uzziah died' hint at that very background: Uzziah had become prideful and decided to burn incense inside the Inner Court of the Temple. Some priests, courageously confronting him as he took up a censer within the consecrated area, were stunned to see signs of leprosy break out on his forehead.

Now *honour* and *glory* are basically interchangeable words in this discussion because the one Hebrew word, 'kabod', covers them both.

In addition, the gifts and offices of God are irrevocable.[33] Apparently Leviathan hasn't lost this office of guarding the glory of God. It seems, if we trespass in regard to God's honour, Leviathan doesn't escort us gently away but lashes out with its savage tail[34] or its incendiary mouth.[35]

Like the reckoning that struck Uzziah so swiftly, so it can take us down in an instant. It's important to recognise Leviathan's role in the created order. As a seraph, it was a throne guardian—or a threshold guardian—and it was charged with protecting the honour and glory of God. Even in its fallen state, it apparently still holds this office of defending honour.

So this gives us the background as to why Leviathan is able to retaliate against us when issues of dishonour arise. And it's not just God's honour that Leviathan has in its protective sights: because we can also criticise Him by showing contempt towards His creation, Leviathan doesn't restrict itself to direct affront on God.

You may have heaped dishonour on your boss; despised your colleagues; ill-treated your spouse or children; harboured a secret hatred towards your parents; or even come into agreement with dishonour that has been heaped on you by becoming convinced you must have deserved it. Leviathan's not choosy: self-dishonour is sufficient grounds for retaliation. If you're looking for some really heavy-duty backlash, you can score a bullseye in that area by reviling the satan or one of his minions. Or even, to a lesser extent, by mocking the government.

God's kingdom is one of courtesy and honour. And He wants us to align ourselves with the values of His kingdom by honouring and glorifying Him above all. But honouring and glorifying Him also involves respecting others. That doesn't mean keeping quiet in the face of abuse, injustice, hypocrisy or lies. Tolerating such behaviour is not honouring to God, to victims or even to the perpetrators themselves. Rather it's complicity with the darkness operating through them.

The last verse of Job 41 tells us Leviathan is king of the sons of pride. The Hebrew word there for *pride*, 'shachats', only occurs twice in Scripture, both times in Job. Such rare words always raise questions about the accuracy of the meaning. Translators have obviously chosen to see 'shachats' as most closely related to 'shachal', *lion*. Hence the translation: *pride*.

Now this might be right. On the other hand, 'shachats' might be from 'shachaq', *laugh, dust* or *pulverise*, or even from 'shachar', *dawn, black* or *seek early and diligently*. Certainly laughter is a strong possibility since the description of Leviathan as *frolicking* in the deep could well be translated *laughing* in the deep.[36] It's an ambiguous word: sometimes referring to *mockery* and sometimes simply to *joyful fun*. It's also a threshold-related word and, when it has overtones of mocking ridicule, is often symptomatic of the presence of Ziz, the spirit of forgetting.[37]

This is not to say that *dawn* and *pride* are wrong. Leviathan's gaze is described as *'like the eyelids of the dawn.'* (Job 41:18 ESV) So perhaps it's meant to resonate with all of these and evoke *lions* and *laughter*, *dust* and *dawn*. Now this combination raises the strong possibility the *sons of pride* are the angelic princes who rule the nations. Scripture calls them *principalities* and sometimes *young lions*.

Canaanite mythology recalls seventy princes, 'young lions', sons of the goddess Asherah. Throughout Israel's history, the people were repeatedly warned about bowing to Asherah poles and worshipping 'She Who Walks On Water'. They were cautioned about her sons who allegedly lived on a mountain fastness to the north of Israel and whose court was the '*assembly of the gods*'.

When Jesus walked on water, He was confronting Asherah, 'Mistress of Serpents'. On the same day as He did this, He reclaimed the 'Bread of Heaven' title from her consort, Tammuz. Later, declaring war on the young lions, He headed up into their mountain sanctuary and into their high council. Peter testified that:

> *He received honour and glory from God the Father when the voice came to Him from the Majestic Glory, saying, 'This is My beloved Son, in whom I am well pleased.' And we ourselves heard this voice from heaven when we were with Him on the holy mountain.*
>
> 2 Peter 1:17–18 BSB

It's often overlooked that the Transfiguration of Jesus is the mind-blowing fulfilment of the prophecy of Psalm 82: God stands up in the '*assembly of the gods*' and declares judgment on them. Effectively, Jesus interrupts a war council!

And just so we don't miss the significance of His action, on coming down the mountain, Jesus appointed seventy disciples to go out into the 'small villages' of a foreign country: to the 'young lions' of the nations. His actions are all devised around massively clever wordplays: the Hebrew word, 'kephir', means both *small villages* and *young lions*.[38]

Leviathan was a highly placed courtier in the heavenly realm. To understand his position, let's look at his counterpart in the natural world: the Levites.

And *yes* there is a connection between the names 'Levite' and 'Leviathan'. 'Levi' means *join*, just as the first two syllables of 'Leviathan' do. This is not coincidental. The Levites were the landless priesthood whose calling it was to live in the midst of the tribes and thereby *join* society together as well as *join* the people to God. Leviathan was to join together the seventy spiritual princes, the shepherd-angels of the nations, under his rule so they would serve both God and humanity. Instead he rules a rebel empire.

Of the many books about Leviathan, perhaps the most famous is Thomas Hobbes' advocacy of social contract.[39] Written during the English Civil War, it argues that 'the war of all against all' could only be avoided by strong, united government—one that, unlike our present system, does not divide church and state. The symbol of

Leviathan, the *joined* and *joining monster* is altogether appropriate for such a proposal. When the body politic is imaged as Leviathan, we realise that such a government would be a counterfeit to both the Levites and the Body of Christ, the joined living stones.[40]

Once we realise the role of Leviathan shadows the role of the Levites, we can move into a deeper understanding of the symbolism surrounding this mysterious creature. I want to focus on just two of the verses we've already looked at:

> *You broke the **heads** of Leviathan in pieces, and gave him as **food** to the people inhabiting the wilderness.*
>
> Psalm 74:14 NKJV
>
> ***Smoke** billows from his nostrils as from a boiling pot over burning reeds. His breath sets **coals** ablaze, and flames pour from his mouth.*
>
> Job 41:20–21 BSB

The key words in these two verses are *heads*, *food*, *smoke*, *coals*.

As we think of these terms in relation to the Levites who alone were permitted to minister within the Inner Court of the Temple, we should be reminded of the three ritual objects within that sanctuary:

- the seven-headed menorah

- the food—the Bread of the Presence—set before God for a week before being given to the sons of Aaron to eat

- the smoke and coals of the altar of incense

The emblems of Leviathan indicate it discharged its offices in the chamber before the throne of God, just as the Levites discharged their offices within the Inner Court of the Tabernacle and Temple.

Leviathan therefore is not just a monster of the deep, not just a fiery winged seraph, not just a twisting coiling serpent—it's also the representation of a place. On earth, the shadow of that place was given to the Israelites as the Inner Court of the Tabernacle.

But what are the implications of Leviathan as the representation of a place? God put His name and His mark on the land of Israel; where has Leviathan put its name and its mark?

Actually Leviathan would like its name and mark on the entire world, but in some places the landscape already invites its continuing presence.

Prayer

Father, there are times when I think I know better than others. That my way is the 'right' way. I step onto a pedestal and, from my high position, I look down on others and I think that what they do and say is, at best, second rate.

Just as often, I live in a dank and dark dungeon and I am loath to venture outside. When I do, I often walk straight into peril and so I hurry back to the comparative safety of my dungeon. I am very aware that neither of these ways is Your way. Nor is combining them—building my high pedestal inside the dungeon so I can look down on my fellow sufferers.

Father, I admit that all of these attitudes are sin. I admit that they keep me from passing over the threshold and coming into the destiny You have called me to, time and again.

Leviathan is very pleased with my failure to repent. While these attitudes are in place, Leviathan rarely has to do anything. I am my own worst enemy.

Father, thank You for the freedom You have given me to choose differently today. I want to love You, love others, honour You and honour others. But even my best efforts are full of hidden vanity, pride and self-serving pity. I am sorry I have dishonoured You by dishonouring myself and others. I repent of thinking I am 'better than' others and I also repent of thinking myself 'less than' others. It is not for me to decide the gifts You've given are inferior or superior. You and You alone are the righteous Judge.

I ask Jesus to empower the words of repentance I have just spoken so I can truly turn my life around, change my heart and honour *everyone*. Out of the love that spills from heaven to me, I ask for Your help to love You back, please You, honour You and glorify Your name.

In Jesus' precious name. Amen.

4

Sight, Smell, Taste

I WAS WALKING ACROSS A PAVED SQUARE in front of a town hall in Northern Ireland when I suddenly heard the voice of God—

God: Speak peace into this spot.

Me: Huh?

God: Speak peace into this spot.

Me: Is that You, Lord?

God: Speak peace into this spot.

Me: *This* spot? This *exact* one I'm walking across now?

God: Yes. This one right here.

Me: Umm... Lord, perhaps You've heard of 'The Troubles'? I'd just like to bring to Your attention the extreme likelihood I'll get arrested if I stop and, umm, loiter. Even if it is for prayer.

> Pause, while I'm desperately trying to regroup my thoughts and come up with a plan.

Me: Oh look! There's a coffee shop just over there! Can I speak peace to this spot from the coffee shop?

God: Yes. That's a good idea.

Me: Phew!

So, for the next half hour, while sipping a cup of coffee, I spoke peace into a specific spot just outside the walls of Derry in Northern Ireland. The square I was praying over was right in front of the town hall. To be honest, I felt powerless. My prayer was unfocused and haphazard. There was no sense of potency in it; I was instead beset with an oppressive feeling of inadequacy.

I'd probably have forgotten this prayer, consigning it to the long list of those with unknown and unknowable outcomes, but a few days later when I was back in Australia, I happened to walk into my mother's loungeroom just as the news came on. I immediately recognised the spot caught on camera. 'It's my *spot*!' I exclaimed.

The following news item was about a gathering in front of the Derry town hall. People had assembled to hear details of a report, 12 years in the writing,[41] into the start of 'The Troubles' 38 years before.

The reporter at the scene spoke of rising anger, as decades of lies and cover-up were finally exposed. It seemed likely the fury would spill over into one of the violent riots Derry was infamous for. But then, sounding confused, the reporter indicated that the crowd was simply dissipating. People were leaving the area in peace.

God wants peace for Northern Ireland. In 1972, fourteen men in a civil rights march were murdered by British paratroopers. They were unarmed and many were shot in the back. Young boys who'd seen their friends killed that day reacted by joining the IRA. The savage sectarian backlash that followed was eventually to claim over 3600 lives.

I was pretty naïve in the days I spoke 'peace' into that specific spot. I knew it was about healing the land. However I didn't realise for some years that, in my head, peace was simply 'absence of conflict'. God had to remind me eventually that, by 'peace', He meant *shalom*, and that in fact I was quite clueless when it came to understanding what that meant.

So, fortunately for me, although I'd been completely inadequate to the task He asked me to fulfil, Jesus is not. This is always such a reassurance to me—it's not the quality of my faith that makes any difference to God, it's that of the faith of Jesus. It's not the quantity, either. I could have faith so wide it stretched across an ocean and so deep it would reach to Mars and back, but that wouldn't impress God either. He responds to the faith of Jesus, my mediator, who takes my feeble, pathetic attempts at prayer and presents them to the Father with amazing power and grace.

Scriptural *shalom* is far more than absence of conflict— it's health, wholeness, integrity, completeness, soundness, welfare. *Peace* in Hebrew implies amends have been made, justice has been done, recompense has occurred.

In fact, *recompense* is probably the word to sum it all up.

Recompense is the flip side of the coin of retaliation. Recompense has positive overtones, retaliation negative. Recompense means that justice has been served and what was damaged or stolen has been restored; it means our inheritance has been returned; it means we can receive the rightful reward of our own labour and of the generations before us.

So it should be no surprise Leviathan is mentioned in connection with inheritance. When we put Isaiah 27:1 into context, this becomes immediately apparent.

> *In that day, the Lord will punish with His sword—His fierce, great and powerful sword—Leviathan the gliding serpent, Leviathan the coiling serpent; He will slay the monster of the sea. In that day—sing about a fruitful vineyard: I, the Lord, watch over it; I water it continually. I guard it day and night so that no one may harm it.*
>
> Isaiah 27:1–3 NIV

The image of a vineyard here is a picture of our inheritance. God directs us to sing to it! Because He mentions it straight after His promise to deal with the spirit of Leviathan, that suggests to me we have to deal with the dishonour in our lives before we can sing to our inheritance, or speak any restoration into this world God asks us to heal.

It's all too easy to reframe this promise of prosperity and think it's about wealth. It's about land and landscape, the mending of the world and the healing of its people.

True peace cannot arrive until justice is done. That's the long history of Northern Ireland: the greater the coverup, the deeper the sense of injustice grew, the more brutal the violence.

Preachers of the nineteenth century were notorious for hellfire-and-brimstone sermons. They often emphasised God's justice to the point where their congregations got the impression He was a cosmic policeman. His omniscience meant He knew each and every infraction of the law we'd committed and He was swift to write out a ticket for wrongdoers to be carted off to hell—unless, of course, they happened to appeal to Jesus.

To correct the imbalance of this kind of theology, preachers of the twentieth century began to emphasise God's love. Make no mistake, there are plenty of people who need this message; plenty who think of God, not as a loving Dad, but in the image of Leviathan—swift to retaliate and slow to bless. There are many who read the words of Jesus, *'Which of you, if your son asks for bread, will give him a stone? Or if he asks for a fish, will give him a snake?'*[42] and think: 'That describes it perfectly. God really will give me a stone if I ask Him for a fish.'

But this miserly image is nothing like God. But neither is the tolerant version who is so forgiving that repentance is really a harsh and unnecessary formality. God surely wouldn't shame us into admitting we were wrong! After all, He's full of mercy and lovingkindness.

Without a well-adjusted view of Him as both loving and just—without a view of grace as empowerment to overcome sin rather than cover it up—then abuse of all kinds will creep in. The history of both church and secular institutions in the twentieth century has shown this, over and over again. When we move away from an insistence on repentance as one of the two arms of reconciliation—the other being forgiveness—we set in place the perfect breeding ground for violence and abuse.

God is not like Eli, the high priest of Shiloh, who lined his sons up, gave them a lecture on the way they were taking advantage of their offices, but didn't follow up his words with decisive action. Judgment fell on the House of Eli for his neglect of the sexual exploitation, physical violence and spiritual abuse by his sons. It involved a curse for his dishonour of God.

> *'Why do you scorn My sacrifices and offerings? Why do you give your sons more honour than you give Me?'*
>
> 1 Samuel 2:29 NLT

For generations to follow, lives were repeatedly cut short as retaliation was visited on Eli's descendents. The massacre of the priests of Nob is one such instance. In one way we can attribute this tragedy to the conflict between David and Saul but the severity of Saul's reaction to finding out the priests have—quite innocently—helped David is inflamed by the defiling curse that follows the House of Eli.

This is such a strong curse that, when I came across a modern parallel—a story of a senior pastor whose son served in the same church and who was accused several times of rape by different women in the congregation—I wondered if it still operated. The senior pastor did not discipline his son even though, in addition to the rape accusations, there were rumours of multiple affairs as well as evidence that the son had appropriated large amounts of money for non-existent ministries. Now the name of the pastor was sufficiently famous to be able to google the family. And sure enough, there were a couple of tragic and heartbreaking news articles about lives in the third generation being cut short in chilling accidents.

When we honour our children more than we honour God, we give Leviathan not only massive legal rights but also very specific ones: most of our descendants will be cut off in or before their prime, and even those who survive will not escape unscathed. They will go blind and their hearts will be broken.

Heartbreak in Scripture doesn't mean a disastrous romance: it means a wound to the very core of our being.

Eli suffered blindness; he died from a coronary attack on receiving the heart-stopping news both his sons had been killed. Likewise, I imagine, soul-wrenching disappointment tore apart the lives of Samson's parents because, although they were devout and God-fearing, they didn't fear Him enough. They too elevated their son to a position of greater honour than God.

Some of us don't make this mistake. But there are plenty of other errors waiting to trip us up. We can honour our parents more than God. Or we can honour our friends, brothers or advisors more than God.

> *'Now in those days the advice Ahithophel gave was like that of one who inquires of God.'*
>
> 2 Samuel 16:23 NIV

Ahithophel was David's advisor—effectively his prime minister—who betrayed him during the civil war with Absalom. Ahithophel was more than a trusted counsellor, he was apparently one of David's nearest and dearest friends. He is probably the person referred to in this verse:

> *Even my close friend in whom I trusted, who ate my bread, has lifted his heel against me.*
>
> Psalm 41:9 ESV

The term *'lifted his heel against me'* means that he's made a choice to ally himself with another.[43] Most commentaries describe Ahithophel's actions in immensely harsh terms. They compare his disloyalty with that of Judas—which is natural, since Jesus Himself quoted this particular verse as a prophetic of Judas' act of betrayal; and, in addition, both Ahithophel and Judas hanged themselves.

Some commentators go so far as to say Ahithophel was a malicious and perfidious turncoat who savagely dishonoured David by assisting Absalom to scheme against him. Perhaps, however, the situation is more complex than bald-faced treachery. It's quite possible David wasn't as innocent as he appears and that, in fact, he was reaping a fairly typical consequence for dishonouring another man's family.[44] There's a very strong chance that Ahithophel was Bathsheba's grandfather! What is more natural than for the head of a family to feel that the entire clan had been dishonoured by the king's violation of his granddaughter's marriage bed? When the chance for revenge presented itself, it seems like he took it: his advice to Absalom carries eerie echoes of David's adulterous behaviour with Bathsheba when she was still Uriah's wife.

That's the problem with dishonour: we want to whip it straight back where it came from. And, while we're busy out-lashing each other, we're unfortunately drawing the dragon-eyed attention of Leviathan.

I feel sad for Ahithophel. His best friend rips his entire family apart by having an affair with his granddaughter. He gets her pregnant, then arranges to have her husband murdered. Is this the behaviour of a best friend? Is this the behaviour of a man after God's own heart?

And how on earth does this best friend—even though he's a king—come to expect that all will be forgiven and forgotten? How do the other families who were torn apart by his fall into temptation—all those mothers and fathers, wives and children grieving the loss of the fine young warriors sacrificed as collateral damage to cover up a murder—how do they feel about the fact the king mourned for a bare week before receiving God's forgiveness?

Isn't this totally unjust?

Of course it is. But it wasn't up to Ahithophel to be the agent of God's vengeance. The law of sowing and reaping would have taken care of the consequences of David's sin without any intervention from an aggrieved grandfather.

The same is true in our lives: the law of sowing and reaping works towards an inexorable end. This law was originally meant to increase blessings throughout creation and upbuild the world in love—but now operates against us.[45] Because of the Fall, it multiplies sin and death, alongside holiness and life. Our only hope of intervention into this cycle of destruction is the power of the Cross of Jesus as it is applied through repentance and forgiveness.

Personally I've come to believe that the law of sowing and reaping is the reason why we're told never to dishonour fallen angelic princes but instead ask God to rebuke them. Think about it: if our 'sowing' is to ask God to tell off His angels for over-stepping the mark in carrying out their offices, what will our 'reaping' be?

What are the natural consequences of such behaviour, spiritually speaking? Why, it'll be that they ask God to give us a warning that we're over-stepping the mark when it comes to our calling! What a marvellous result! What more could you ask for?

I've encountered many people who, even knowing this, still find it difficult to say, 'May the Lord rebuke you!' or 'Lord Jesus, please rebuke this spirit!' Rather, they say: '*I* rebuke you!' to the spirits. Using presumed authority, they avoid going through our mediator Jesus and instead choose to tackle entities such as Leviathan directly.

We should always be deferring to Jesus and the Holy Spirit, who are the Source of our authority. When we flaunt Scripture, we dishonour Them; and when we exceed the bounds of the authority given to us, we show disrespect.

There is a great and common misunderstanding of the words of Jesus:

> *I have given you authority to trample on snakes and scorpions and to overcome all the power of the enemy; nothing will harm you.*
>
> Luke 10:19 NIV

These words refer to spiritual powers, as the next verse makes clear. The specific mention of 'snakes and scorpions' tells us that it's not low-level demon foot-soldiers that Jesus is talking about but mighty cosmic entities like Python and Leviathan.

But this authority doesn't mean, as some people think, that we can do just as we please in spiritual warfare. It means rather that we have all of the Lord's backing to enforce *His* commands. We have been delegated authority to uphold the Word and the will of God; it is not a sanction to enforce our own decrees.

For me, the hardest times to obey when I'm in spiritual warfare are in another country—and when I'm right at the place the Lord has impressed on my heart for many years—and He says: 'No! *No*, you can't pray here.'

When I've waited ten years for that particular moment, come thousands of kilometres and when I know the chances I will ever return to that place are miniscule, I'm tempted to go ahead anyway. But fortunately, God puts a physical obstacle in the way. It's never an insurmountable obstacle but it's a sufficient deterrent to make me pause and ask God for the way forward. And when, instead, He tells me to walk away, that's so hard. I've a lot—sometimes a vast and deep lot—invested emotionally, intellectually, spiritually, and sometimes financially.

Given the passage of time, I can look back and see what I was too invested at the time to realise: I didn't have any authority—which I knew—but I hadn't been granted any permission either. I'd had a 'good' idea, not a 'God' idea. And, as mentioned previously, there's a huge difference:

> *The Holy Spirit had prevented them from preaching the word in the province of Asia*

> *at that time. Then coming to the borders... they headed north for the province... but again the Spirit of Jesus did not allow them to go there.*
>
> Acts 16:6-7 NLT

It was certainly a 'good' idea to preach the gospel in the province of Asia. But it wasn't a 'God' idea; God wanted Paul and Silas, as it turned out, to move into Europe. There they encountered the spirit of Python and were, in my view, bested by it.⁴⁶ It was a salutary lesson. Much later in Corinth—the gateway to Python's most famous shrine—Paul was prepared with God's tactics for overcoming it—tactics that were a far cry from his fleshly methods back in Philippi.

When we are praying for the healing of the land, we will always be in confrontation with Leviathan. There are several reasons for this:

First, land is inheritance. The return of inheritance is recompense: the gift of *shalom* through restorative justice. As we have seen, when God overcomes and pierces Leviathan, He will give us the vineyard—the inheritance—that we are called to sing over.

Second, the nations have been claimed by Leviathan. Just as God has put His name and His mark on the land of Israel to signify her people as His own particular possession, so has Leviathan put its name and its mark in many places.

Third, this is evidenced in Scripture. But unless we are familiar with the geography of Israel and the countries round about her we will miss the patterns given in the text. Moreover, these geographical waypoints seem to reflect the spatial arrangement of the Tabernacle. So let's look at that in order to orient ourselves.

The area under consideration is the Inner Court. After passing through the door into this sanctum, the Levites—and only the Levites—carried out their ministrations in the Holy Place. Because it was a sacred area, they went bare-footed. A heavy, embroidered curtain at the far end, opposite the door, cordoned off the Holy of Holies. There the Ark of the Covenant was kept. Only the High Priest could pass through this curtain on the Day of Atonement.

Within the Inner Court were three items of furniture: the seven-branched menorah, the table with the twelve loaves of the Bread of the Presence, and the fragrant altar of incense where prayers were offered.

- The seven-branched menorah corresponds to the seven heads of Leviathan.

- The bread corresponds to the pieces of Leviathan provided as food for the people.

- The smoke of the altar of incense corresponds to the smoke rising from the nostrils of Leviathan.

THE TABERNACLE

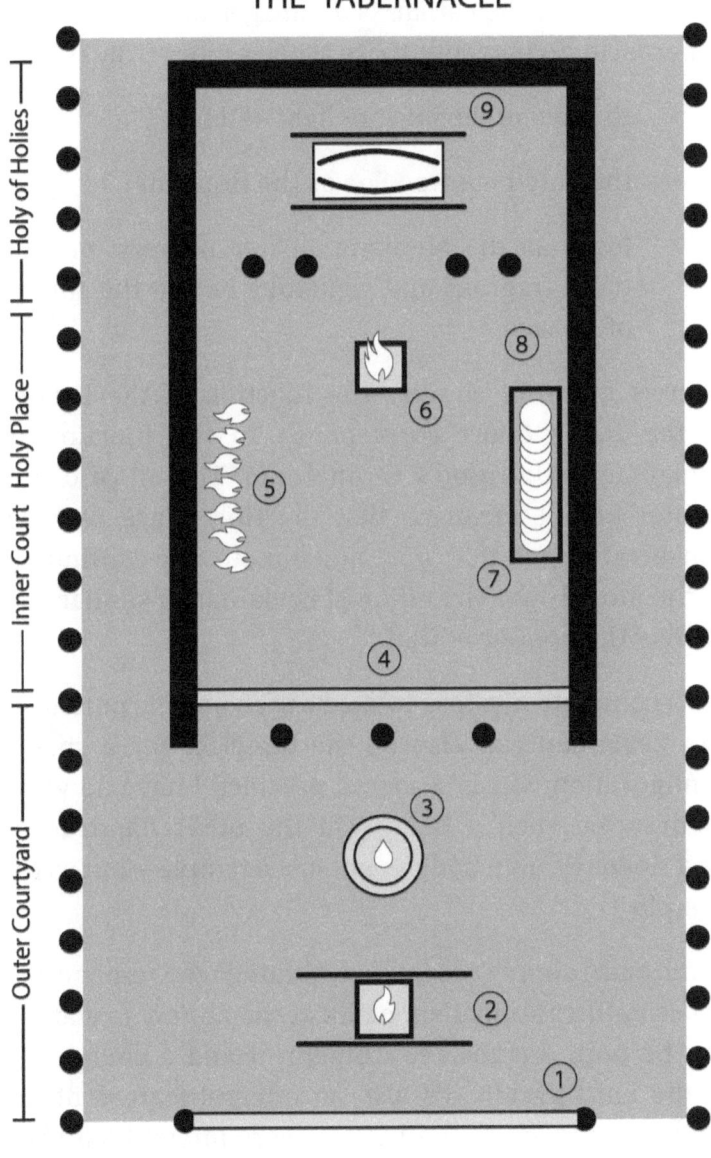

① Gate
② Altar of Burnt Offering
③ Laver
④ Door
⑤ Menorah
⑥ Altar of Incense
⑦ Table of Shewbread
⑧ Veil
⑨ Ark of the Covenant

Now, of course, Leviathan is an imager of God, as is the Tabernacle. So in reality, these aspects more truly reflect:

- the sevenfold Spirit of light and fire
- the only-begotten Son as the Bread of Life
- Jesus as the Mediator of our prayers, making them fragrant and righteous before the throne of Heaven

There's more, of course. The function of the Levites in the Inner Court corresponds to the function of Leviathan within God's throneroom. The office of the Levites entails ensuring that the Holy Place remains consecrated, and that glory and honour rise continually to the Most High. The office of Leviathan is similar—to protect the honour of God.

It's a complete mystery to me how an angelic potentate like Leviathan can also be the template for a spatial configuration within a sacred precinct. I have no word to describe such a being. On the other hand, Jesus described His own body as not just a temple—but as *the* Temple.

In the end, I simply accept that, although the remnants of my scientific rationalism baulk at the notion, Leviathan can be both a creature, a blueprint and a counterfeit of the Lord's body. It's also an integral feature of the landscape, much as the Levites were integral features, living on the land, as part of life in the clans and villages of Israel. Leviathan is a 'joining' aspect, much as the Levites 'joined' together the tribal confederation through shared worship of Yahweh as they performed their priestly duties.

The image of Leviathan in Thomas Hobbes' seminal work of the same name is of a body politic—a necessary monster joining the people of a nation in a social contract. Hobbes' vision for a new system of government is a strange paradox. Despite his deep Christian devotion, he seems not to have noticed that his proposed 'Leviathan' is a counterfeit of the Body of Christ—the priestly assembly foreshadowed by the Levites.

A more contemporary symbol of Leviathan is an image suggested by Mark Sayers: the submarine *Nautilus* from the classic novel *Twenty Thousand Leagues Under The Sea.* The joined, impervious monster of the deep has become a riveted, tightly-sealed underwater craft.[47] In this age of mechanisation, entertainment and isolation, Sayers perfectly adapts the ancient iconography of Leviathan to our current world: we as God's chosen people, royal priesthood, holy nation and particular possession have become as inflexible as a metal submarine, as ignorant as the amusements that divert us, and as proud as a puppet of doing things our own way.

But the Body of Christ is meant to be a wise and supple marvel, completely surrendered to our Head. The human body is a physical, sensory structure; and our senses are important to experiencing delight, wonder and beauty in life. In the Inner Court of the Tabernacle, there is a focus on three human senses—sight, taste and smell.

- *Sight*: the light of the seven-branched menorah is an aid to sight
- *Taste*: the Bread of the Presence, which remained for seven days on the table, before being eaten by the descendants of Aaron
- *Smell*: the incense from the altar where prayers were offered

Symbolically, these indicate *vision*, *appetite* and *discernment*.

Once again, there are parallels with Leviathan along with the realms of heaven. More significantly, there are parallels in the world around us—in the landscape, in the geographical marks, in the thresholds and boundaries, in the names.

One of the most interesting Scriptural examples showing Leviathan within the landscape occurs in the story of Elijah. He had taken refuge at the brook Cherith. There he was fed, at God's command, by some ravens. When the brook dried up, God told him to leave:

> *'Go at once to Zarephath in the region of Sidon and stay there. I have directed a widow there to supply you with food.'*

> 1 Kings 17:9 NIV

When Elijah found the widow, she was preparing her last meal. She had only a little oil and some flour left, but Elijah prophesied:

> *'The jar of flour will not be used up and the jug of oil will not run dry until the day the Lord sends rain on the land.'*
>
> 1 Kings 17:14 NIV

And so it proved.

Now oil meant *light* to the Hebrews; in fact the generic word for *oil* relates to the *sun*. Oil was the power source for the light of the menorah. And flour, of course, makes bread—like that of the Bread of the Presence.

By themselves, the flour and the oil—even with the blessing of God—don't indicate that Elijah has entered a sacred space. But together with the other information provided, they rise in status.

The brook Cherith flows from the east down a deep-sided wadi into the Jordan River. So on leaving here and travelling north into Phoenician territory, Elijah was entering present day Lebanon. He was heading to a coastal town, now known as Sarepta, half way between the ancient trading ports of Tyre and Sidon. The name 'Zarephath' means *smelter, forge, furnace, metal-working, gold-smithing* or *crucible*—all of which neatly reveal its industries. It also specialised in glass-blowing and that art, though now dying, is still practised there today.

Nevertheless, its modern name 'Sarepta' shows the root meaning more clearly. Behind *smelter* and *furnace* is the word 'seraph'—those six-winged angelic entities who cry, 'Holy! Holy! Holy!' and who have a name meaning *fiery serpent*.

In heading up the Phoenician coast to Zarephath, Elijah would at some point have had to cross the Litani River. This waterway is named after Lotan, the seven-headed water monster of Ugarit religion—and the Canaanite equivalent of Leviathan.

A river is a boundary, a natural threshold, and in ancient times the 'pass over' of such places might well involve covenant—just as entering a house and 'passing over' the cornerstone would raise a threshold covenant. Certainly when the Israelites led by Joshua 'passed over' the Jordan, it was considered a covenantal action which they immediately ratified by circumcision at their first camp.

Cherith, the name of the brook where Elijah had taken refuge, meant *cut*. It naturally evoked *covenant* because, in those days, a covenant was *not* created or made, it was *cut*. As Elijah left for Zarephath, he moved across the landscape as if walking through the different areas of the Tabernacle. He passed through a river boundary that corresponded to the separation between the Outer Court and the Inner Court. And there he stayed: he remained within the glory. At the Lord's direction, Elijah had reached sanctuary in a place that, foreign as it was, imaged the sanctum of God's throneroom.

In the natural world, the name 'Zarephath' pointed to a place of metal-working and ore-smelting, but in the spiritual realm it meant *place of the seraph* or perhaps, utilising a little rhyme, *dragon prince of the doorway*.[48] Given the town's proximity to Tyre, the Phoenician stronghold of the guardian cherub who was expelled from the mountain of God, perhaps that poetic licence is not unwarranted.

However there's one unusual aspect of Elijah's journey. Shouldn't he have been going to Zarephath to meet a priest, not a widow? Perhaps that peculiarity was meant to foreshadow the incoming of the Gentiles. After all, centuries later, Jesus retraced Elijah's steps and also met a needy woman in this same region. All she wanted was the crumbs that fell from the Master's table.

Prayer

Loving Father, help! I don't want to disobey or dishonour You; I don't set out to do either deliberately but it *just* happens. I am not spiritually aware of Your presence and I fail to see the world as You see it, nor do I experience life, myself and others as You see us all.

Lord, open my eyes to the beauty that surrounds me. Open my spirit to the peace and contentment of hearing Your voice singing over me and over my inheritance. Open my ears to Your songs in the night. Open my heart to receive Your love.

Lord, I confess that I am reaping what I have sown. I admit that in my busyness I am blind to Your extravagance. Your songs of wonder, joy and refreshment which I once heard in early childhood have been silenced for many years. My heart has hardened and closed off by my go … go … go. I am no longer a human being. I have become a human doing.

Forgive me, Lord. Tune me once again into the heart of Jesus. Whether He cradles me with a lullaby or sets me to march at His drumbeat, cause me to cherish His song so that I grow up *into* Him, not grow up *beside* Him. And whenever I step off-track I ask the Holy Spirit to cover, hover over and protect and remind me and draw me back into Jesus.

Thank You, Father, for what You have given me. Thank You, Jesus, for what You have done for me and thank You, Holy Spirit, for Your ever-present presence in my life. I am indeed blessed beyond measure. And I resolve that, by the empowerment of Your holy grace, I have been blessed to be a blessing.

In the name of Jesus of Nazareth. Amen.

5

Forensic Accounting

HONOURING OUR LEADERS IS incredibly important. It doesn't matter whether they are noble and show deep concern for the people and the advancement of the nation, or whether they're immoral, unrighteous and seek nothing but their own advantage. God has appointed them.

> *It is God who alters the times and seasons,*
> *and He removes kings and promotes kings.*
> *He gives wisdom to the wise and knowledge*
> *to the discerning.*
>
> Daniel 2:21 ISV

In honouring our leaders, we honour God's choice for us. And when we dishonour them, we set ourselves up for retaliation. Let's take a close look at a Scriptural example.

After the death of Saul, the first king of all Israel, a time of civil war followed. The supporters of David fought it out with the faction loyal to the House of Saul.

Eventually, after a fallout between Saul's son and his army commander over some mutual dishonour—what else?—support for the House of Saul evaporated. David became the uncontested king. But then the harvests failed, year after year after year.

> *There was a famine for three successive years; so David sought the face of the Lord. The Lord said, 'It is on account of Saul and his blood-stained house; it is because he put the Gibeonites to death.'*
>
> 2 Samuel 21:1 NIV

Now, if you've been involved in praying for your nation, you've almost certainly heard this story. You've been told how, as a result of David's actions in appeasing the Gibeonites, God finally answered prayer on behalf of the land. At least—that's what I've always heard. It wasn't until I was reading Robin Gallaher Branch's masterly exposition of the little-known women of the Old Testament that I realised David didn't solve anything. He actually compounded the problem, making it far, far worse.

The background is clear: Saul had broken covenant with the people of Gibeon and virtually wiped them out. What is often *not* clear is that this is an example of generational iniquity. It was, in many telling ways, a close repetition of the genocide his own tribe had suffered. He simply passed it on—in essence, informing us that he and his people, the clan of Benjamin, harboured hatred and unforgiveness towards their fellow Israelites for the results of the war. A particular hatred seems to have been reserved for the people of Bethlehem who were obviously seen as the instigators of the conflict. So the fact that David the giant-killer came from Bethlehem didn't help matters in any relationship. The tribe of Benjamin was actually so small it couldn't go up against the might of Judah, let alone the entire confederation of tribes. Nevertheless it could vent its frustrations on the vulnerable people of Gibeon who lived in their territory. However in doing so, the people of Benjamin—led by Saul—not only broke covenant, they called down curses on the land.

Now when David realised what the problem was, he went to the Gibeonites and asked them what they wanted. Revenge—that's what they wanted.

This is the point where David made a critical error. When the Gibeonites asked him for permission to execute the remaining descendants of Saul, he should have pointed out that they were asking him to resolve a covenant breach by making another covenant breach. David had covenants with both Jonathan and Saul. Today, most people are aware of his covenant with Jonathan, but not of the one with Saul. However, a covenant is implied by the fact he was Saul's armour-bearer. Now these covenants required that David defend Jonathan and Saul *and their families* to the death.

David fails a significant test at this point. He fell into temptation. And the temptation was a massive one: to secure his throne for life by eliminating the last remaining rivals who might conceivably have a claim on the kingship. He handed over seven males from the House of Saul to the Gibeonites, who sacrificed them—and I choose the word 'sacrificed' advisedly—in an apparent fertility ritual at the start of the barley harvest.[49] Since this is the time immediately after the Passover when the 'first fruits of the barley' are offered to God, David allowed a terrible counterfeit to be enacted within his kingdom.

Still, you'd think, from the many renditions of this story I've heard told in the past that at that point God answered prayer on behalf of the land. But that is to completely excise the most important person in the entire story.

Her name is Rizpah.

She was Saul's concubine and the mother of two of the sacrificed men. Day and night, she kept watch over all the exposed bodies, protecting them from wild beasts and the ravages of weather. Robin Gallaher Branch says she did this for months, until the autumn rains finally came. Now it's not clear that the length of time was for months—but it *is* clear that it was a substantial period. It was long enough for David to realise the focus of the entire nation was on a grieving woman, battling to preserve the last tatters of honour for a family who had been unspeakably dishonoured.

In a culture where respect for the dead required their same-day burial, exposure to the elements was the supreme disgrace. The Philistines had exposed the bodies of Saul and his sons on the walls of a fortress partly for this reason: to heap dishonour on them and on the people of Israel.

Rizpah's name is instructive.[50] It tells us her role in this national calamity.

During Isaiah's vision of God, he lamented that he was a man of unclean lips and lived amongst a people of unclean lips. He was speaking of dishonour and his resultant unworthiness to look upon the face of God. But then:

> *One of the seraphim flew to me, and in his hand was a* GLOWING COAL *that he had taken with tongs from the altar. And with it he touched my mouth and said: 'Now that this has touched your lips, your iniquity is removed and your sin is atoned for.'*

Isaiah 6:6–7 BSB

The glowing, purifying coal that cleansed Isaiah's lips was a *rizpah*.[51] And this is Rizpah's role in David's kingdom: to purify it from dishonour.

David had monumentally mishandled the information God had given him. Instead of negotiating an outcome that combined justice with mercy and also enabled him to keep his covenant with the House of Saul, he botched the situation.

David was an impetuous man, a curious and complex mixture of utmost humility and strange pride. This time of the famine was not the only occasion God's anger was kindled against Israel. Assuming the incidents are arranged in chronological order, the next time it happened was when David ordered a census of the fighting men.

> *The anger of the Lord burned against Israel, and He incited David against them.*
>
> 2 Samuel 24:1 NIV
>
> *Satan rose up against Israel and incited David to take a census of Israel.*
>
> 1 Chronicles 21:1 NIV

The book of Samuel says the census was at God's instigation; Chronicles pins it on the satan. Joab, the commander of David's army, protested vehemently, but in vain. No one could talk David out of it. It took him the best part of nine months to come to the abrupt realisation that Joab had been right all along. The whole idea of relying on the numerical strength of the army was a declaration of distrust in God's promises. It was deliberate dishonour to His Name. Retaliation was inevitable and David knew it. God's mercy was severe: He asked him to choose between three options as to what the retaliation would entail.

Now, because this was a clear-cut case of retaliation, it's much of a muchness as to which account is right about the instigator: God or the satan. In a sense both are right. God was angry at some unspecified dishonour,

Leviathan took the matter in hand and pushed David into a position where he had to take responsibility.

Responsibility was never David's strong suit. When it came to the whole Gibeonite debacle, it was only the wildly obsessive actions of a grief-stricken woman that finally brought him to his senses. He'd dishonoured his covenant with the family of Saul as well as the men themselves. He'd dishonoured their bodies in not allowing them decent burial—and actually, when it came right down to it, he'd dishonoured Saul and Jonathan themselves.

There had never been a time of national mourning for the fallen king or his heir. Thirty days for Moses, thirty days for Aaron, seventy days for Jacob—but none for a leader who, despite his many flaws, had done much to heal the rift in the tribes. Belatedly, David realised he needed to honour not just the bodies of the men killed by the Gibeonites but also Saul and Jonathan.[52]

So he sent to Jabesh Gilead for their bones and had them interred in the tomb of Saul's father—at Zela in the territory of Benjamin—just outside Jerusalem.

It's then—*finally*—that God answered prayer on behalf of the land.

When we fail to realise the importance of honouring our leaders, we put our entire nation at risk. Plague followed David's census of the fighting men; famine came about when a covenant was dishonoured. It's irrelevant that

that covenant should never have been taken out in the first place: it still stood.

This is what we forget about covenants: they survive the death of the people who took them out. They are binding on the descendents of the covenant-raisers. If the descendents violate the covenant, then curses are triggered.

Until we take ungodly covenants to Jesus and revoke them, they are still operational. And the retaliation we experience is not abnormal.

A confirmation of the link between unholy covenants, dishonouring God and the lack of answers to our prayers for healing the land is found in the prophecy of Isaiah:

> *Hail will sweep away your refuge of lies, and water will flood your hiding place. Your covenant with death will be dissolved... Do not mock, or your shackles will become heavier. Indeed, I have heard from the Lord God of Hosts a decree of destruction against the whole land.*
>
> Isaiah 28:17–22 BSB

The 'refuge of lies' spoken of here is, in my experience, the most significant obstacle blocking any possibility of breakthrough in most people's lives. False refuges are used by the enemy to create hidden idols as we seek comfort away from God in times of crisis. As I testified in *Hidden in the Cleft*, a false refuge can be as simple as a cup of coffee. It doesn't need to be big for the satan to use it to frustrate our destiny. In fact the more innocent it seems, the more effective it is.

Because we simply don't notice it.

One reason Leviathan has such a field day with retaliation against believers is that we are so often oblivious to dishonour. We don't notice it in the Scriptural record, especially if it involves the 'designated hero'. We thus fail to join the dots and overlook the straight line connecting dishonour to retaliation. The 'reaping' is invisible to us because the 'sowing' has gone straight over our heads.

David dishonoured a long list of people during his lifetime. However, we're inclined to gloss over almost all of them except Bathsheba and Uriah. Of course, David received a lot of dishonour from Saul—but the point is this: we notice when Saul dishonours others while we tend to overlook the same character flaw in David. Yet his behaviour shows a consistent pattern over many years. He dishonoured his daughter Tamar after she was raped; and dishonoured his son Amnon by not calling him to account for the rape. Perhaps he felt it would be hypocritical to do so; after all, he'd dishonoured Bathsheba, her husband Uriah the Hittite, along with her family including her grandfather Ahithophel who also happened to be his counsellor and best friend. He dishonoured the men who died in the cover-up of the murder of Uriah, as well as their families. He dishonoured Absalom and also dishonoured his troops during the civil war with Absalom—to the point where Joab had to warn him he was about to lose their loyalty. He dishonoured

Joab, as well as the other army commanders, who opposed the census. He dishonoured his sister, Zeruiah, through his constant slighting references to her when he was angry with Joab and his nephews.[53]

This is far from the full list. As we have seen, he dishonoured Saul and Jonathan after their deaths, as well as Saul's family. In addition, he dishonoured Achish who offered him protection from Saul by constantly lying to this Philistine king about his raids; he dishonoured the priests of Nob by lying to them—an action that led to their deaths. And I'm never certain about this last one, but it is sufficiently troubling to my spirit to mention it: did David dishonour the people of Benjamin by setting up his capital at Jerusalem? The city of Jebus which he took was in the territory of Benjamin.[54] Should he have handed it over to them? After all, he belonged to the tribe of Judah. Was conquest enough to give him the rights of possession? I'm not sure.

And if it wasn't enough, how does that dishonour impact the land going forward? Even today?

Now in a significant number of the cases mentioned above, David repented. That was always one of his major strengths: his willingness to repent once his heart was finally convicted.

Because repentance has been so misunderstood in recent years, it's worth spelling out what it is and what it is not. Repentance is *not* agreeing humbly with the accusations of the enemy. *Nor* is repentance agreeing swiftly with the accusations of the enemy.

When the enemy is Leviathan, every accusation is a twist on the truth.[55] If we agree with those distortions, we dishonour God by being complicit with a lie. Leviathan can gain legal rights against us simply through our agreement with its accusations.

Repentance is turning back to God and agreeing with His truth. It's saying sorry to Him and speaking out an intention to keep following Jesus. And it's asking Jesus, through the power of His shed blood, to enable us to fulfil that intention.

Repentance is one of the two arms of reconciliation. The other is forgiveness. If one person in a ruptured relationship extends the arm of forgiveness but the other does not put out the arm of repentance, then it's impossible for true reconciliation to occur.

In many cases involving abuse in church settings, dishonour is rampant. The victim is counselled, sometimes aggressively, to forgive; but frequently repentance is not required of the perpetrator. In many cases, not even an apology is expected, let alone restitution or recompense. Instead, the responsibility for reconciliation is placed entirely on the shoulders of the one needing to forgive. When this happens, it is spiritual abuse and it adds another wound to whatever other abuse has already occurred.

Now Leviathan is *not* the same as the spirit of abuse; nonetheless they often work together. Situations of abuse are rife with dishonour, so it's very important not to compound the contamination by layering more dishonour into the mix. We are called to return good for evil, blessing for cursing, honour for dishonour.

By doing so, we step into *shalom*, into glory, into rest.

Unfortunately idolising an idealised picture of David created by leaders who want to emulate this 'man after God's own heart' establishes an interior attitude that sets up a perfect breeding ground for abuse.

Such idolatry—whether it's given to our leaders or whether it's self-allotted—means that, in any conflict, there's a tendency to demonise the other person. Thus we overlook Saul's good qualities and his immense achievement in unifying the tribes into a working coalition after the internecine war with Benjamin.

Eli honoured his sons more than he honoured God; but some of us honour our political and ecclesiastical leaders more than we honour God. It's a common human failing to want heroes and, having got them, to elevate them to virtual godhood. And once our leaders realise they have the uncritical support of followers and can impose their will without censure, abuse inevitably follows. It's why we need checks and balances, responsibility and accountability.

The agenda of the spirit of abuse is quite different from that of retaliation—yet they work in tandem to prevent us from establishing ourselves once we've passed the threshold. Often we wonder why God doesn't answer prayer. However the testimony of Scripture is that one major reason is dishonour. Peter informs men that one hindrance to answered prayer is a husband's mistreatment of his wife. The story of Saul and the Gibeonites shows us that another hindrance is breaking covenant. But the story of David and the Gibeonites shows that another hindrance is dishonour of our leaders—even if they themselves are not particularly honourable.

> *'Therefore I tell you, whatever you ask for in prayer, believe that you have received it, and it will be yours.'*
>
> Mark 11:24 NIV

No doubt you've often heard this verse quoted about the importance of believing in order to receive an answer from God. But how often have you heard it coupled with Mark 11:25? The very next verse places a condition on that believing. It lets us know why answers to some of our prayers can be detained.

> *'Whenever you stand praying, forgive, if you have anything against anyone, so that your Father also who is in heaven may forgive you.'*
>
> Mark 11:25 ESV

Unforgiveness is a form of dishonour to God. He has forgiven us freely and offered us the riches of heaven, but so often we fail to pass this treasure on.

Now honouring our leaders doesn't ever mean that we should involve ourselves in their dishonour. We do not, as so many people have done in recent times, cover up a leader's sin. Even concealed their crimes!

We called to be like Rizpah, the purifying coal, who showed a king what honour looked like. In doing so, she stood in harm's way for David—at least in a spiritual sense. She minimised the retaliation on the nation for the obscene dishonour heaped on the previous royal family—by the Philistines *and* David!

We are not to dishonour those whom God honours. For in doing so, we dishonour God.

One well-attested attribute of Leviathan is its ability to warp and distort communication. In reflecting on my own experience of such twisting, I realise that one or more participants in any dialogue affected by Leviathan have to be complicit with it through pride or contempt. Both sides talk *across* each other rather than *with* each other.

It's certainly possible to recognise that crooked twisting has occurred in a communication but, unless both sides are committed to honouring the other with truth and transparency, that recognition doesn't usually help. Any request for clarification so that light can be shed on the meaning of words will be met with a slippery response—a response that spirals off on a baffling tangent. Rather than spelling out the matter more clearly, the response will deepen confusion.

This is different from situations involving Python or Ziz.

When Python is involved, the emphasis is on ambiguity and riddles: on veiling the truth, rather than bending it. This means particular phrases will recur in conversations—because the person is not so much concerned with preserving the truth as presenting a message that is *not false*. Ambiguity requires a certain exactness of phrasing.

Ziz, on the other hand, is quite willing to tear truth apart through false accusation or simple memory loss.

Leviathan on the other hand will wrench truth out of shape. Its nature is to coil and twist. We can see this distortion happening throughout Scripture when words are bent out of their original godly intent. For example, 'baal', the *husband* of Israel who betrothed Himself to His people at Sinai, became just one of many baals contending for their worship: Baal Melqart, Baal Hadad, Baal Aliyan,[56] Beelzebul and so on.

Even the name 'Jesus' needs clarification. One of the first questions new converts who've been involved in the occult often ask is, 'When you say, "Jesus is Lord," which Jesus do you mean?' Creeds are despised by many believers but their singular virtue is that we can be very specific: 'Jesus of Nazareth, who suffered under Pontius Pilate, was crucified, died, was buried and rose again on the third day. *That* Jesus!'

When we start to be intentionally clear with our language and transparent in our behaviour, Leviathan will sense danger. It fears being pierced so it will flee if that looks like it's a possibility. This is why, when you try to 'pin someone down' who is cooperating with Leviathan, their return messages fly off on some wild tangent. Leviathan is momentarily fleeing, often to seek its allies.

Is it possible to deal with someone committed to a relationship with Leviathan? No, not really. The twisting will become worse. The coiling of communication will become more entangled.

Yet having said that, there is something we can do to improve the situation. It's like repentance. Only much more intense. I call it 'forensic accounting'. Or sometimes I call it the 'Day of the Lord'.

Genevieve was repeatedly told the same thing by various bankers and brokers. 'You're too old, you're single, you have no guarantor, your credit record is bad, you work only by commission. You've got no stable income.' So they turned her down flat for a home loan.

She was convinced, however, that God had a house for her and a repayment scheme she could afford. So, despite the repeated disappointments, she persisted in seeking out loan brokers to help. One morning, just a few hours before another one was to arrive, she felt a nudge from God. His voice was unusual—not the warm and fatherly tone she knew well; it was more like that of a stern judge.

He pointed out she had a bad credit rating because she'd gone guarantor for her brother many years before. When he got into trouble, she'd been left with the debts and she'd lost everything as a result. She'd blamed her brother for her circumstances for a considerable time, but had long since forgiven him.

However, it wasn't forgiveness God wanted to talk to her about. It was *repentance*.

When, God wanted to know, *did you do the due diligence you should have done about your brother's enterprise? You are the steward of My gifts to you*, He pointed out, *and you failed to act responsibly in relation to them. You blamed your brother for so long but you've never admitted you are just as much at fault.*

Genevieve wept. The conviction she felt at God's words was intense. In the middle of sobbing, she realised that, if she wanted the broker to catch God's vision for her house, she needed to repent of her negligence. That was what God was calling her to do. She'd known what her brother was like but, instead of exercising caution and wisdom, she'd dishonoured the very discernment God had given her. She'd dishonoured God and His gifts to her. She'd treated them lightly.

In Scripture, to treat something lightly is to have contempt for it. Honour and glory are *weighty*.[57] The Hebrew language speaks of honour as being heavy, while dishonour is considered light.

Curiously the English language preserves an almost poetic memory of this connection between lightness and Leviathan. Words like levity (*light-mindedness, frivolity, fickleness*), levitate (*rise by virtue of lightness*), leaven (*something that causes rising*) not only start with similar letters but have overtones reminding us of aspects of Leviathan's nature.[58] This is not to say we should be forever serious or to suggest we should frown on laughter—but to remind us that, with just the tiniest bit of defiling leaven, exuberant joy can become foolish mockery. This is never okay.

Genevieve repented.

The broker later told her he didn't really understand why he'd taken on her case when he considered it hopeless right from the start. But strangely, he became just as persistent as she was. Seven times he applied to different financial institutions, at last finding one that would give her both the loan and the repayment scheme she could afford.

I doubt if I would have understood the true nature of what God had put Genevieve through, except that I'd gone through it myself a few days previously. It began when I stumbled across a Bible verse:

> *The things my people do are as depraved as what they did in Gibeah long ago. God will not forget. He will surely punish them for their sins.*
>
> Hosea 9:9 NLT

I must note that down, I thought. When I come to write a book on the Janissary spirit—the spirit of abuse—that's an important comment to keep in mind. Duly noted, I went about praying for a friend of mine who has an office as watchman in God's kingdom but who had been caught in a trap, specifically targeting this role. I was praying again the next day about this when I had a sudden thought. *I wonder if there's a verse in the Bible about watchmen and traps.* It turns out it's the same chapter of Hosea, just one verse earlier:

> *The prophet is a watchman over Israel for my God, yet traps are laid for him wherever he goes. He faces hostility even in the house of God.*
>
> Hosea 9:8 NLT

How interesting, I thought. *The verses are right next to each other.* But that's all I thought. I didn't even examine the context—not that, at that stage, it would have helped.

The following day I was editing a chapter of a manuscript and the first verse I had to check for accuracy was:

> *When I found Israel, it was like finding grapes in the desert; when I saw your ancestors, it was like seeing the early fruit on the fig tree. But when they came to Baal Peor, they consecrated themselves to that shameful idol and became as vile as the thing they loved.*
>
> Hosea 9:10 NIV

By this stage, I was starting to get the message. Three consecutive verses from the ninth chapter of Hosea in three days. Not a coincidence. Each day for the next week, I read that chapter over and over trying to work out what God was saying to me. Finally, I came to a conclusion. It was a very uncomfortable one, given that the thrust of Hosea's prophecy at that point was clearly about the Day of the Lord.

I said to God: 'I'm guessing You're trying to tell me something about the Day of the Lord. But I'm also guessing that You *don't* mean the Great White Throne Judgment at the end of time. So I'm therefore guessing that You want to do something like Jesus mentioned in the Parable of the Unjust Steward.'

> *There was a certain rich man who had a steward, and an accusation was brought to him that this man was wasting his goods. So he called him and said to him, 'What is this I hear about you? Give an account of your stewardship...'*
>
> Luke 16:1–2 NKJV

'Yes,' said God. 'You've got it.'

My heart sank. I was horrified. I couldn't imagine anything I'd like to do less.

'Let's just call it "forensic accounting",' God went on.

And so began a session in which God took me through my part in an ongoing problem of several years' duration. It involved passing information about several instances of abuse that had been reported to me onto a person higher up the chain of command. Over a long period of time, I began to suspect none of these issues had ever been dealt with; perhaps had never gone beyond the person I had alerted about them. Actually, I wasn't sure of the protocol for going further. And that was where things got messy.

However, as God took me through the choices I'd made across the years at various critical moments, He kept repeating one thing: I had failed to exercise due diligence. I had never checked with the person I'd reported to on the progress of the matter I'd raised with them. I'd been lazy and distracted but—most of all—I'd been a people-pleaser concerned for how it would look if I asked about what was going on. Would I appear nosy, intrusive, prying, nagging or officious? I'd failed to exercise due diligence because I'd put other people's perception of me above the hurts of those who'd told me their stories. At the end of the day, I'd extended far too much trust—the kind that should be given only to God Himself.

It was harrowing. Sitting down with God and forensically analysing the choices I'd made was an experience I never ever wanted to repeat. But fortunately it prepared me for the next phase in the situation. Because, as I later discovered on investigating how Christian organisations respond to reports of abuse, there's an almost universal response at the point when their negligence is uncovered. It's a demand for trust. There is no evidence of repentance, just a unilateral ultimatum involving a requirement that trust be shown through no more questions being asked.

Now the spirit of abuse is not the same entity as Leviathan, although both are threshold guardians. However, it's easy to see how they hook up to produce a toxic situation: when someone demands trust in circumstances like these, they're asking you to honour them by dishonouring God and others.

While we are to '*honour one another above ourselves*' (Romans 12:10), we are never called to mock God in the process.

A few months later, God said to me, 'I want you to render accounts again.'

I'd made another perfect mess of a situation I'd got myself into when I'd chosen to rescue an author who'd botched the publication of her first book. This woman didn't know enough about margins in the publishing industry to induce any retailer to stock her book. She was also unaware of various legal requirements within the industry. Even as I took pity on her ignorance, I wondered if it was fleshly pity I was exercising, not godly compassion.

The situation was so unpleasant by the end, with various accusations flying, that I wasn't entirely surprised when God asked me to front up for another session of forensic accounting with Him. But the thought of another 'Day of the Lord' with His laser-like focus analysing all my personal choices in this particular episode was unbearable. I couldn't face it. For almost six weeks, I resisted. Every time God brought it up, I fled from His gaze.

Finally, one morning I woke up and surrendered: 'Oh, alright. Let's do it. *Quickly. Right now*. Before I change my mind.'

This time turned out to be immensely different from the first. It was freeing and refreshing, releasing and revitalising. As God pointed out the pivotal moments of choice in all that had happened, it became clear that, had I made any other decisions, everything would have turned out worse. *Much worse.*

In *Prince Caspian*, the sequel to CS Lewis' classic children's fantasy, *The Lion, the Witch and the Wardrobe*, the Great Lion raises an interesting point. 'To know what would have happened, child?' said Aslan. 'No. Nobody is ever told that.'

Now, while many people agree that we can never know what would have happened if we'd made other choices at critical moments, I disagree. Quite profoundly. We may not be able to see into the far future and where that will land us but, generally speaking, we can see how things would have panned out in the immediate circumstances.

And as we go to the Lord, render accounts to Him and subject ourselves to a personal 'Day of the Lord', we find ourselves visited by one of God's 'Suddenlies'.

Just as Genevieve found herself suddenly supported by a broker who had no intention of telling her anything other than that her case was hopeless, so we too—when we've rendered accounts and repented of those choices that were less than wholesome—find the situation has changed. As swiftly as a lightning bolt.

As I took my own situation to the Lord, I said to Him: 'Honestly, I don't think there were any good choices in what I faced. Whatever I did would have been wrong.'

God was in agreement with me. 'Yes. Much of life is on that level.'

I didn't think God got it. 'But then *what* do I *do*?'

'Repent.'

'You mean, Lord, that whatever choice I'd made, I'd have to repent of it?'

'Yes.'

I thought about this for quite some time. 'To say that, when there are no good choices, you should make a choice anyway and then repent of it sounds twisted. Like pre-meditated sin. Even abuse of grace.'

'What other option is there?'

That was an excellent point. When doing nothing is wrong, and every alternative is varying degrees of bad, we have to make the best choice we can with the knowledge we have. As a result we tend to make excuses, absolving ourselves of responsibility. The forensic accounting that comes with a personal 'Day of the Lord' strips us bare of self-justification regarding our own actions. The fact that we chose the *least* bad option is irrelevant, it was *still* bad. Rendering an account for our stewardship forces us to acknowledge our own part in adding to the pain of a bent world—even if that position was basically 'damned if you do and damned if you don't.'

Our repentance as a result of this accounting paves the way for the Suddenly—a very favourable one. We aren't guaranteed this, but God's gift of grace—*repentance*—often has remarkable side effects.

Yet sometimes lack of repentance paves the way for a Suddenly of a different kind.

The story of Ananias and Sapphira illustrates a fatal Suddenly.

> *Now a man named Ananias, together with his wife Sapphira, also sold a piece of property. With his wife's full knowledge he kept back part of the money for himself, but brought the rest and put it at the apostles' feet.*
>
> *Then Peter said, 'Ananias, how is it that Satan has so filled your heart that you have lied to the Holy Spirit and have kept for yourself some of the money you received for the land? Didn't it belong to you before it was sold? And after it was sold, wasn't the money at your disposal? What made you think of doing such a thing? You have not lied just to human beings but to God.'*
>
> *When Ananias heard this, he fell down and died. And great fear seized all who heard what had happened. Then some young men came forward, wrapped up his body, and carried him out and buried him.*
>
> *About three hours later his wife came in, not knowing what had happened. Peter asked her, 'Tell me, is this the price you and Ananias got for the land?'*

'Yes,' she said, 'that is the price.'

Peter said to her, 'How could you conspire to test the Spirit of the Lord? Listen! The feet of the men who buried your husband are at the door, and they will carry you out also.'

At that moment she fell down at his feet and died. Then the young men came in and, finding her dead, carried her out and buried her beside her husband.

Acts 4:36–5:11 NIV

Normally as we approach a threshold, we receive a test. It happened for Jesus: three times He was tempted in the wilderness by the spirit of Python. It happened for Paul: as he took the gospel from Asia to Europe, he encountered the spirit of Python in Philippi. It happened for the people of Israel: as they left Egypt and came to the Sea, an entire cabal of spirits were waiting for them. Again, when they were approaching the Jordan crossing forty years later, the spirit of Python and others turned up again.

A threshold test happens for all of us. It can be when we transition into something new or transition out of something old. For Ananias and Sapphira, it was giving up the security of the property they owned and handing over the money. Here we have our own tests writ large: on the threshold, we will be asked to make a sacrifice by Python.

As Peter said, they didn't have to hand over *all* the money. In fact, they didn't have to hand over *any*. It was theirs to do with as they chose. However they wanted the praise and honour they'd undoubtedly seen Barnabas receive for his contributions to the common good.

Now, in those days, purchasing land wasn't as simple as it is today. The buyer and seller would walk the land together, often watched by half the locals, as they haggled and negotiated their way towards a deal. The finalisation could take months and was mostly conducted in the public eye. So, to keep the closing price confidential, Ananias and Sapphira would have had to have involved the buyer in their conspiracy.

Their actions exemplify the three different kinds of sacrifice normally offered on a threshold to spirits like Python. Typically these are:

(1) sacrifice of others

(2) sacrifice of self

(3) sacrifice of the honour of God

By securing the complicity of the buyer in their scheming, Ananias and Sapphira sacrificed his integrity. They also sacrificed their own integrity, as well as their honour. To gain honour, they forfeited it first. To gain public praise, they chose private duplicity.

Self-sabotage is exceedingly common on a threshold. While it's possible to pass over the threshold by sacrificing others, it's not possible to do it by self-slaying. That's the ultimate in counter-productive choices.

How do we know if we're prone to the sacrifice of self? One of the most significant indicators is when we are able to say: 'I don't know why I did that! I *never* do things like that! And of all the times to do it—just as I'm about to front up for an interview for the job I've been waiting for all my life!'

On the other hand, if we've sacrificed others on the threshold, Python or Rachab may accept our offering and allow us entry into our calling. After all, sacrifice of others always entails dishonour. We're perfectly set up for backlash by Leviathan.

Ananias and Sapphira, however, chose the third option: sacrificing the honour of God. We do this when we claim to be followers of Jesus but flaunt our immoral or unethical practices publicly. Or alternatively we do it when we hide our faith in order to land a job, sometimes justifying this choice by thinking our witness will be all the greater if we secure the position.

Why do such fatal Suddenlies occur? Why doesn't God intervene to save us?

> *Now I want to remind you, although you once fully knew it, that Jesus, who saved a*

> *people out of the land of Egypt, afterward destroyed those who did not believe.*

> Jude 1:5 ESV

Jude, half-brother of Jesus, wrote these words. They are not tempered by heart-warming encouragement; they are a blunt warning. Once we cross the threshold, we are in dire danger: we can now be guilty of treachery.

Enemies, by their nature, cannot be betrayed. But friends can.

If we pass over a spiritual threshold, we come into a covenant with the spirit of the place. The nature of this covenant includes hospitality, friendship and mutual defence.

When we look at the Scriptural passages where a fatal or almost-fatal Suddenly occurred, we can see a strong and prominent pattern involving breach of threshold covenant. For example, when God tries to kill Moses on the way to Egypt, it's because he has been treacherous in entering a lodging place on the way. When thousands of people die after worshipping the golden calf, it's not simply because it's an idol, it's because of the violation of the threshold covenant made when the seventy elders dined with God on His sapphire banqueting floor. When Jeremiah proclaims the final destruction of Jerusalem by Babylon and Zedekiah's capture, it's because the people have made a covenant with God to set their slaves at liberty and then, as soon as the immediate crisis passed, rescinded it.

When we dishonour God through covenant breach, we step out from under the covering He has set over us. Leviathan thus has a perfectly free hand.

The Jewish people of today have coined a word for sudden reversals orchestrated by God: 've'nahafochu'. It's associated with the Purim festival, featuring the story of Esther and its unexpected flip in the fortunes of the Jews of Persia—one day about to be slaughtered, the next given the power to attack their persecutors.

This beautiful word, 've'nahafochu', means: *And everything was turned upside down.*

Hope deferred makes the heart sick. And hope long, long deferred goes further: it makes the heart forget that Scripture is full of moments of 've'nahafochu'—the sudden reversals of God.

I'd got so used to God taking years to answer my prayers that He had to jolt me out of my expectation it would take decades to see any result. It happened on the tarmac of the airport in Tonga. I was travelling with my friend, Janice. The plane we were in was refuelling on its way from Rarotonga to Sydney—a stop that was normally unnecessary. However, there was not enough aviation fuel to make the long haul to Sydney. The plane was being diverted to Auckland—which was very awkward since I had an appointment in Sydney the following day.

Janice and I, comparing notes later, both had the same question for God: 'Is this retaliation from Leviathan for our prayers in Rarotonga?'

God gave us both the same answer through a return question: 'What did you pray for?'

'For the cutting of ungodly supply lines.'

'As in the natural, so in the spiritual,' God said.

'You know,' I said to Him, as it dawned on me that physical supply lines had indeed been cut, 'I've got used to waiting *decades* for answers to prayer. Next time You plan to answer *immediately*, could You let me know?'

God is the Lord of Ve'nahafochu and we, who are called according to His purpose, inherit a special lineage and legacy.

We carry His grace and blessing, and we are sent forth to turn the world upside down.

What should we do when the threshold guardians demand a sacrifice at the doorway into our calling? What other options are there besides sacrificing others, sacrificing ourselves or sacrificing the honour of God?

The fourth option is that of whole-hearted faith. It means standing firm, looking the intimidating monsters in their mesmerising eyes and announcing, 'Jesus is the all-sufficient sacrifice for every threshold. He is my covenant defender who has paid the price in His blood for me to access my calling. Please stand aside. I'm coming through.'

At this point you might find Python cackling with laughter or Leviathan snortling with mirth. Ziz might be rolling in the aisle or Rachab exploding with hilarity. Because it's one thing to *say* the words and entirely another to *believe* them. And the threshold guardians have a fair idea what's in our heart when it comes to faith in Jesus.

I'd been suffering from a virulent skin rash for several months and nothing seemed to alleviate it. Now I believe that illness is a threefold cord: physical, psychological, spiritual. So, to examine the spiritual thread, I looked for skin disorders in Scripture. There they are frequently associated with grumbling, back-biting and speaking ill of other people. I did a lot of soul-searching. Finally I said to the Lord that I didn't think I was doing this in relation to others—in fact I thought quite the reverse.

In a particular situation at the time, the people involved were grumbling, back-biting and speaking ill of me.

It seemed to me I was indeed reaping—but not the consequences of my own sin, rather it was that of others.

How this reaping was being foisted onto me I didn't know, but it could only be by occult means. More importantly, if this was so, what was it *in me* that caused such a curse to alight?

Much much *much* more importantly, I wondered whether I was thinking this just to avoid being held accountable for dishonouring others. Was this some deceit of my heart that provided me with a justification for blaming others? I'd not long been through the first episode of 'forensic accounting' with God and I didn't want to make that distressing experience null and void by failing to take responsibility for my own actions.

So I took the situation to God: 'Look, I don't like what I'm thinking. And I definitely do not like thinking what I'm thinking about people I have deeply respected in the past. I don't even know what to call this kind of inversion, if it exists. If I am right—and I am actually reaping what other people have sown—could you please send me some objective evidence? And preferably someone to tell me what this is called?'

Just a few days later, a couple of friends told me a mysterious story which culminated in the question: 'What's sin-eating?'

'I think it's in a book by Francine Rivers. Not sure otherwise.'

Wikipedia to the rescue: 'A sin-eater is a person who consumes a ritual meal in order to spiritually take on the sins of a deceased person. The food was believed to absorb the sins of a recently dead person, thus absolving the soul of the person. Sin-eaters, as a consequence, carried the sins of all people whose sins they had eaten.'

As I read this, I realised it was the answer to the question I'd asked God. 'Sin-eating' was a way of describing *reaping what others had sown*.

As I looked into this further I realised that, although the responsibility for passing off the reaping for sin wasn't mine, I was liable for accepting it. I had usurped the role of Jesus as 'Saviour'; I had—yes, fleshly pity tempting my heart once more—fallen into the trap of believing that Jesus needed help to be the all-sufficient sacrifice for the whole world.

I repented as soon as I realised what I'd done. And when I woke up the next morning, the rash had almost completely disappeared. Overnight I was healed. Leviathan's legal rights were removed when I stopped trying to add to the atonement of Jesus. Sin-eating—and its close spiritual kin, disease-eating—dishonour Christ and His accomplishment on the Cross.

My mother once had a close acquaintance who suffered from a serious and very painful auto-immune disease.

One day, while they were lunching together with a couple who had a healing ministry, the acquaintance mentioned this problem. The minister, Tom Jewett, immediately asked what line of work she was in and if she was empathetic. She replied that she was a chaplain and was very empathetic.

'That's it!' Tom exclaimed. 'Empathy is sin. We are called to be compassionate—not empathetic. We are to *suffer with* the other—*not enter into their pain* by being empathetic.'

He took her away for prayer and, just half an hour later, she returned radiant, all smiles, and pain free. The next day she walked a kilometre—something she hadn't done in years.

All was well—for about six months. But old habits die hard and, back working in chaplaincy, she began to slip into empathy again. The auto-immune disease returned.

Now you may not agree with Tom Jewett about empathy being sin. It could well be a question of how to define 'empathy'.[59] But his point, that we are *not called to enter into the pain* of others—thereby usurping the role of Jesus and trying to help Him out with the atonement—is a valid one.

This is an easy trap to fall into: even a thinker as notable and perceptive as CS Lewis was ensnared by it. Influenced by his friend, Charles Williams, who thought following Christ involved a life of substitution and exchange,[60] Lewis considered there was no coincidence in the fact he was mysteriously losing calcium from his bones just at the time his wife, Joy Davidman, who was suffering from cancer so desperately needed it.[61]

There is absolutely no doubt we are called to bear burdens for other people and sometimes sacrificially so. However there are spiritual thresholds we should never cross: we should never allow our burden-bearing to become sin-bearing, sin-eating or disease-eating. In extreme cases, we can even carry the dishonour for an entire region or country. This is to arrogate the atoning work of Jesus.

If we love others, we will allow Jesus to serve them, not stand in His way.

Just as Leviathan is apt to go overboard in addressing dishonour, so we can be tempted to go overboard in burden-bearing, and cross a forbidden line. We are not called to share in the sin-burden of others, we are called to be righteous and holy through the atoning blood of Jesus.

Dishonour comes in so many shapes and forms. And it's tempting to think that it is honour that overcomes Leviathan. It's certainly helpful, but at the end of the day, honour is simply not a fruit of the Spirit.

Way back in Eden, the fruit of the Tree of the Knowledge of Good and Evil was weaponised to enable the serpent to claim our inheritance. So naturally, because the principle of 'sowing and reaping' is an immutable law, then we have to be able to reclaim that inheritance through weaponised fruit.

We're not used to thinking of the Fruit of the Spirit as weapons. Instead, we've got used to thinking that an increase in faith and authority is the answer to almost everything when it comes to spiritual warfare. But faith doesn't overcome Python, the spirit of constriction. Love does.

And faith doesn't overcome Ziz, the spirit of forgetting. Joy does.

Nor does faith overcome Rachab, the spirit of wasting. Patience does.

Yes, the missing one in that line-up is *peace*, shalom. And that is what overcomes Leviathan. Not honour but, as you've probably suspected for several chapters, *shalom*.

The first time we hear of God as '*Yahweh Shalom*' is during a name covenant[62] between the Lord and Gideon. An angel turned up as Gideon was threshing wheat in a winepress while hiding from the Midianites. The Israelites were so thoroughly dispossessed of their inheritance so often and so profoundly that the raiders were thought of as locusts.

It's no coincidence that Gideon gave God the name '*Yahweh Shalom*' (Judges 6:24) at this time: although it seems ironic, since Gideon has just been commissioned to go to war, the naming[63] is in response to a promise that inheritance will be restored, that justice will prevail and that the Israelites will soon enjoy the work of their own labour, rather than having it taken from them by marauders.

Dealing with these spirits is so often fraught with difficulty because what works to overcome one of them will not work for the others.

Often we aren't even aware that we've neglected to go to God and ask Him for a specific, personalised, bespoke strategy to fit our unique circumstances and the particular spirit we're currently battling. Instead of following the Lord's tactical plan, we've copied some tried-and-true method that worked in the past. Now, in fact, sometimes these methods didn't actually work *for us* but we've heard they worked *for others*. So, with faith in the plan, we try it out. But faith in the plan is not the same as faith in God.

Besides, an increase in faith is not the answer to every battle in life. The only Person who knows the strategy that will work successfully for you is the Captain of the Hosts and your battle-companion, the Paraclete. So it's vital to consult with them.

They might actually say that we are so ill-prepared to go up against the enemy that we don't have permission. It might be that dishonour has created such a solid legal foothold for Leviathan to retaliate against us that we first of all have to deal with that issue.

Or it may be that we haven't dealt with issues of justice and restitution. We can't lob the fruit of peace at Leviathan until it's ripened and matured. And for that to happen, making amends is a pre-requisite. That's not always possible but we can attempt to do so.

Recall that *shalom* is not simply peace but health, wholeness, integrity, completeness, soundness, welfare. One word to sum this all up is *recompense*. Remember that I described recompense as the flip side of the coin of retaliation? Recompense is positive, retaliation is negative. As mentioned previously, in Hebrew, recompense implies amends have been made, justice has been done, fairness has prevailed, righteousness has been called forth, compensation has occurred.[64]

We can't get *shalom* without these things—and therefore we can't get it without honour. We can't receive recompense until we are willing to first recompense others. Since our true inheritance includes *shalom*, we can't receive that inheritance while we are denying justice to others.

It's the old golden rule.

> *'Do to others as you would have them do to you. For this is the essence of the Law and the Prophets.'*
>
> Matthew 7:12 BSB

Here Jesus has re-framed the 'sowing and reaping' law, shifting its usual emphasis on negative consequences towards more pro-active and positive outcomes.

Just simply honour others by treating them the way you'd like to be treated yourself. Easy as.

Or is it?

What about when someone deliberately dishonours us? It's one thing to say 'treat them the way you'd like to be treated' but how does that work in practice?

Jesus gives us a clue: *'If someone slaps you on the right cheek, turn to him the other cheek also.'* (Matthew 5:39 NIV)

Bob Gass comments on this statement: 'In Jesus' day, society was built around shame and honour. The left hand was considered unclean; it was not to be used for eating—or for hitting. So a blow to the right cheek would be done with the backhand. It was a way to publicly insult someone. A backhanded slap was something done only to a social inferior, such as a slave or a child. So when someone insults you, what should you do? Everyone expects one of two responses: retaliation or cowering. Jesus is saying, "Your safety and your honour are in the hands of your heavenly Father." So now we get creative. One possibility is that we could turn the other cheek. Our enemy can't backhand our left cheek. Either he has to fight you as an equal, which he doesn't want to do, or he has to find a nonviolent way to resolve the conflict. So, who do you get insulted by? "Slaps" often take the form of barbs, digs, and backhanded comments. Someone demeans your idea at work. Someone accuses you falsely at home. A relative says something judgmental about you. What is your first instinct—retaliation, fear, or both? With the Holy Spirit helping you, there's a new possibility. Don't run and hide. Don't strike back. Confront the other person with honesty and strength. Be creative, patient, and active. Lovingly work towards reconciliation.'[65]

When it comes to dishonour, Jesus isn't actually telling us in this verse to accept abuse and line up for it a second time. That's a misunderstanding of meekness. Rather He's saying to confront the abuse in an honouring, creative way. And if you can't? If the abuser is using physical, emotional or spiritual violence to succeed in getting their own way and is unwilling to genuinely repent of the harm they're causing?

The spirit behind this is not Leviathan, but Belial—and God tells us we are to separate ourselves from those influenced by this particular spirit. God is intolerant of abuse—it looks nothing like love. But His people are all too often ready to accept it in their midst.

Now when you're in a situation where simple and straightforward dishonour has been heaped upon you—not abuse, for that's a different category—it's time to say to the One who has promised us He will be our paraclete and cover our back, 'How can I honour this person while standing up to them at the same time? How can I bless them with *shalom*? How can we live at peace together?'

For love and peace are what Jesus asks of us.

> *'If it is possible, as far as it depends on you,*
> *live at peace with everyone.'*
>
> Romans 12:18 NIV

> *'Blessed are the peacemakers, for they shall*
> *be called the sons of God.'*
>
> Matthew 5:9 NKJV

Jesus promised that God would bless peacemakers, not peace-lovers. My mum tells this story:

> For several decades my favourite Scripture was Matthew 5:9—*'Blessed are the peacemakers—they will be called children of*

God.' And you've probably guessed from this that I considered that I was a peacemaker. I even reminded the Lord at times that I was His 'Number One Peacemaker'. I was quite sure there was no one else alive quite as good at it as I was.

Then one day I'm sure I heard Him say: 'Dell, you aren't a peacemaker.'

'Waddayamean?' I asked Him. 'I'm your Number One.'

'No, you aren't,' He told me. 'You have turned avoidance of conflict into an art form. At the first sign of conflict you flee the scene. That is *not* peacemaking.'

'Oh!' I realised the Lord was right. He shattered my illusions—as well as a few delusions—that day. I'm still not good at handling conflict but these days I no longer call it 'peacemaking'. I love peace but I realise I still have a tendency to appease and to freeze, instead of negotiate a reconciliation.

Peacemakers pay a price—they have to engage with those involved in conflict to try to bring about reconciliation; they have to intentionally mediate, not fight or flee, freeze or fawn.

Shalom-makers, on the other hand, have an even deeper work to do. For shalom-makers, it's not simply about reconciliation but about health and wholeness, honour and restoration.

Back towards the end of the last century, I contracted parvovirus. My kidneys were on fire; I drank eight litres of water in an hour; I was so sick I simply fronted up to the nearest doctor. She took one look and diagnosed parvovirus as one of the three possibilities for investigation. The blood tests came back and that's what it was.

Just a few weeks later, she got married and went to Jamaica. Then the fun began. Because every doctor I saw after that point-blank refused to believe in her diagnosis. *Human beings*, they said, *do not get parvovirus. It's a dog disease.*

In the school where I worked, eleven cases of parvovirus affecting staff or their families occurred in the next few years. But my doctors steadfastly maintained it was impossible. Now the main observable symptom of parvovirus is difficulty in moving. Getting out of bed took twenty minutes. Basically, it felt as if my body, from the hips to the knees, was 'locked' in position. A bout of parvovirus knocked me flat and it took most of a year to reasonably recover.

In a period of seven years, I had four recurrences of the disease. And then my dad got cancer. He wasn't given much hope by any doctor so he decided to try alternative medicine. He sent me off to do a course in German New Medicine.[66] Now the basic tenet of this system is that all disease has physical, psychological and spiritual components. It theorises that, generally speaking, all disease starts with a sudden trauma and then follows a similar pathway. Within that pathway, there are particular crucial moments: some of which are physical, some psychological and some spiritual. Nevertheless to become truly well again, truly restored to health, there is a secret ingredient in whatever medicine you need to take.

That secret ingredient is *forgiveness*.

Now, from the time of the sudden trauma to the time you're first likely to notice some sort of onset of a disease is around two or three years. Just as a seed doesn't produce fruit overnight, neither does a disease accelerate to full-blown maturity. It takes a 'season' of growth. But still, what constitutes the 'seed' that we plant in our lives at a traumatic moment? The 'seeds' are words.

What words do we speak over our lives in a moment of shock? What do we say, automatically and unthinkingly, that comes from the deep recesses of our hearts? What statement did we plant, just like a seed, that would take around two years to become a fully fledged disease?

You see, viruses are around us all the time. If eleven people associated with my school got parvovirus over a space of two years, then it was around my school a lot. But only some people contracted it, others didn't. What made some susceptible and others not?

According to Dr Hamer who originated this theory, the problem wasn't really the words we spoke at the time of the trauma. Those words were really the symptoms. Behind them, in the deeps of our heart, were the reasons we spoke those words. And those reasons always go back to some wounding early in life. We have not forgiven those who hurt us. We may even have forgotten the incident involved, but that only makes forgiveness harder.

Now the pathway of disease outlined by Dr Hamer is full of significant and critical moments. As I compared it to my bouts of parvovirus, I realised that they fitted the pattern extremely well. Although parvovirus was not described in any German New Medicine book, I felt the basic principle was to look at the effect of the disease and what it prevented me from doing. Easy enough analysis: it stopped me from moving.

So I asked myself: *When did I say, 'I can't move,' about two years prior to the first onset of parvovirus?*

I was stunned to realise I could think of the moment immediately. It was during the breakup of a friendship. Someone close to me had decided to put conditions on our friendship and had spelled them out in some detail. Feeling trapped by the sudden restrictions, I burst into tears and said, 'I can't move.' Some of the conditions were: never help, never offer to help, never ask whether help is needed, never get anyone else to help.

But what else do friends do but help their friends? 'I can't move' was my expression of the feeling that to be a friend I had to act as if I were *not* a friend.

As I thought further about the attacks of parvovirus, I could think of an 'I can't move' moment about two years prior to every instance. So I sat down and made a list, going all the way back to my childhood, of times I felt trapped and couldn't move. And, with some help from a couple of counsellors, I realised I had a split between my identity and destiny that had begun with a traumatic event in early life. There were many layers of forgiveness to work through.

Not long after working through this, my breakthrough event happened and I told my story to a woman who laughed at me. She mocked the idea that a virus was empowered by the words we spoke over ourselves. 'I had polio when I was five,' she said. 'Are you trying to tell me I said, "I can't walk" when I was three?'

Her face suddenly changed and her eyes grew wide. 'Oh! I can see myself. It wasn't "I can't walk!" it was "I *won't* walk!" I remember being so angry with my family. I was furious. I remember saying to myself I'd show them.'

The tongue has the power of life and death. The tongue has the power of illness and health. But simply declaring healing and wholeness is not going to cut it, though many believers would like to think it does. This woman changed her entire perspective after this and would never let a single negative word about health pass her lips. However she continually dishonoured people, not through destructive words but through dominating control. She was aggressive in demanding people be shunned and locked out if they'd spoken words of doubt about anyone's health.

But words of faith are not the arbiter of health, although many believers like to think they are. Our faith does not usher in the wholeness and welfare of shalom. Rather the faith of Jesus as He intercedes for us does so. Forgiveness and repentance, restitution and justice are vital aspects of reversing the negatives we've spoken over ourselves and the diseases we've made ourselves spiritually susceptible to, but they are grace-gifts to be allied with the atoning work of Jesus.

Shalom partners with love and joy, patience and kindness, goodness and faithfulness, gentleness and self-control. They are the fruit of the Tree given for the healing of the nations.

A Prayer for Shalom

Heavenly Father, great Father of Lights whose Son Jesus is our peace, Your Word says:

> *You will keep him in perfect peace whose mind is stayed on You, because he trusts in You.*
>
> Isaiah 26:3 NKJV

Help me trust in You. Help my mind to be anchored in You.

Father, Your Word also says:

> *The Lord gives strength to His people; the Lord blesses His people with peace.*
>
> Psalm 29:11 NIV

Thank You for blessing me with peace and with strength. Help me trust in You. Help my mind to be anchored in You.

Father, Your Word continues with the words of Jesus:

> *Peace I leave with you; My peace I give you... Do not let your hearts be troubled and do not be afraid.*
>
> John 14:27 NIV

Thank You for the peace Jesus gifted to us. May He still my heart and calm my fears, as once He stilled the storm. Thank You for sending Him to this troubled world. Thank You for blessing me with peace and with strength. Help me trust in You. Help my mind to be anchored in You.

Father, Your Word says this also:

> *The peace of God, which transcends all understanding, will guard your hearts and your minds in Christ Jesus.*
>
> Philippians 4:7 NIV

Thank You for Your promise that my heart and mind will be guarded by a peace that transcends all understanding. Help me to stop focusing on the worries of the day but on Your love, mercy, kindness, goodness, justice, faithfulness. Guide me into my inheritance and calling. Help me to recognise Your provision, Your healing, Your resources for me. Show me what is robbing me of Your peace. I surrender to You, Lord, and commit myself to fulfilling what You ask of me. Thank You again for the peace Jesus gifted to us. May He still my heart and calm my fears, as once He stilled the storm. Thank You for sending Him to this troubled world. Thank You for blessing me with peace and with strength. Help me trust in You. Help my mind to be anchored in You.

In conclusion, Your Word says this:

> *Let the peace of Christ rule in your hearts.*
>
> Colossians 3:15 NIV

May it be so to Your honour and Your glory. Thank You for Your promise that my heart and mind will be guarded by a peace that transcends all understanding. Help me to stop focusing on the worries of the day but on Your love, mercy, kindness, goodness, justice, faithfulness. Guide me into my inheritance and calling. Help me to recognise Your provision, Your healing, Your resources for me. Show me what is robbing me of Your peace. I surrender to You, Lord, and commit myself to fulfilling what You ask of me. Thank You again for the peace Jesus gifted to us. May He still my heart and calm my fears, as once He stilled the storm. Thank You for sending Him to this troubled world. Thank You for blessing me with peace and with strength. Help me trust in You. Help my mind to be anchored in You.

In Jesus' Name I pray: Amen.

6

Chaos and Enchantment

TINY BREADCRUMB TRAILS THROUGH SCRIPTURE lead to unexpected places as we try to build a profile of Leviathan.

'Rizpah' isn't the only word for *live coal*. There's also 'resheph', derived from 'saraph', *burn* or *live coal*, which has the same Hebrew spelling as its intimate relation, 'seraph', *six-winged angelic being*. Besides *live coal*, 'resheph' can also be translated as *lightning*, *fire-bolt*, *flashing arrow*, *spark*, *burning fever* or *plague*.

Now it happens an obscure Canaanite deity by the name of Resheph[67] was a godling of plague, war and thunder—and his name is considered to originate in this Hebrew word.[68] Besides bringing pestilence, Resheph also allegedly had the power to heal disease.

Until I came to write this book, I'd never heard of Resheph. Yet as I gathered information on this entity, I quickly realised Jesus had conducted an all-out, no-holds-barred war against it. I also started to suspect

Leviathan might well be Resheph under another name. But rather than complicate the question of identity in these pages, I've generally sidelined any discussion of Resheph for a companion volume.

The big question about Leviathan is this: is it the 'satan'? Actually, it's not easy to be sure. The 'satan' is simply a title meaning *the adversary, the opponent, the arch-enemy*. It doesn't really indicate which specific antagonist. So, although we've got used to the traditional assumption that the 'satan' is the same entity every time it's mentioned in Scripture, that doesn't automatically follow. Certainly every reference could be to the same being, but there's also the possibility we are facing different enemies at different times. The Book of Enoch, for example—which was so popular at the time of Jesus and is quoted in the epistle of Jude—mentions many satans.

So is it actually possible to identify the 'serpent' of Eden? The actual Hebrew word is 'nachash'. For many commentators this indicates Leviathan. And certainly that's a strong possibility, given the crafty twisting[69] applied to God's words. However the curse that God speaks over the serpent—with its mention of *heel*, culturally referring to *choices*[70]—appears to me to apply more readily to Python. In addition, the exploitation of ambiguity seems to fit Python better. And while these two are the most obvious contenders, they certainly aren't the only ones. The spirit of forgetting, Ziz, has a part since Adam doesn't correct Eve's mistaken words about touching the tree. Nor does he comment on her omission of Yahweh in the name of God.[71] His passivity is extraordinary, since he was with her the whole time.[72]

There's no certainty the conventional identification of Lucifer[73] with the serpent of Eden is valid—or that the anointed cherub of Ezekiel 28 who was expelled from the mountain of God is identical to the 'light-bearer'.

In fact, we've bundled up the various threshold guardians, as well as other fallen spirits, into a single entity called 'the satan', 'the devil'[74] or 'the enemy'. We have to be very careful not to attribute to these separate beings the sort of unity that rightly belongs only to the Godhead. And we have to be extra careful not to talk about the Father, the Son and the Holy Spirit in a way that suggests more division between their Persons than we do when we talk about the fallen angelic creation.

My personal belief—and I stress it's only my opinion—is the 'serpent' of Eden represents a cabal of spirits who conspired together against humanity. All the unholy threshold spirits were involved. So although I agree with those who believe the most likely candidate for the actual 'serpent' is Leviathan, I nevertheless think it was acting on behalf of a diabolic group of plotters.

Now not only was Leviathan a key player in the garden at the beginning of time, it also re-emerges in a similar role at the end: it's the most likely suspect for the seven-headed dragon of the Book of Revelation. Recall that it's the king—perhaps 'emperor' would be more appropriate—of the principalities, a cohort of seventy angelic majesties or 'young lions' or 'shepherd-kings' who govern the nations.[75] Since it reigns over those entities who maintain spiritual watch and oversight of the human rulers of this world—it would, naturally, like to style itself 'king of kings', the title that belongs to Jesus alone.

> *On the part of the robe that covered His thigh was written, 'King of Kings and Lord of Lords.'*
>
> Revelation 19:16 CEV

The Hebrew word for *dragon* is 'tanniyn'. Its first syllable is the word for *water monster*.[76] As we've seen, this element 'tan' or 'than' occurs in Leviathan and Nechushtan. It also occurs in Lotan, the Canaanite equivalent of Leviathan, as well as Python, another threshold spirit. It crosses a cultural barrier and pops up in the Maori word for *monster*, taniwha. Generally speaking these are chaos monsters, so the gigantic titans of Greek mythology from which we derive the word *titanic* might well be part of this pattern.[77] The chief Germanic deity, the warlord Wotan (also called Woden or Odin), also includes this segment as part of his name.

And let's not forget that satan contains this syllable too!

Once we recognise these tanniyn as chaos-bringers, it becomes abundantly clear why shalom is the particular fruit of the Spirit that overcomes them. In Hebrew, shalom is spelled shin-lamed-vav-mem. Shin, the second-last letter of the Semitic alphabet, is drawn with three prongs and represents *teeth*; lamed represents a stylised *shepherd's staff*; vav denotes *a hook*; and mem stands for *the sea*. However, more abstract concepts were hidden in letters as well. Teeth symbolised *destruction*; a staff symbolised *authority*; a hook symbolised *attachment* and the sea symbolised *chaos*. Thus one translation of shalom is *destroyer of authority attached to chaos*![78]

shalom

peace

mem vav lamed shin
sea hook staff teeth
chaos attached authority destroy

> PEACE *means* to destroy the authority attached to chaos

Another Hebrew word apparently related to 'tanniyn', *dragon*, is 'tannur', *oven*. Because, although these words relate to *chaos-bringing water monsters*, many of them also relate to *fire-breathers*.

Common modern names that include this syllable are: Jonathan, Tania, Nathan, Ethan and Tane.[79] As noted in *God's Priority*,[80] such names testify to unresolved dishonour in the family line.

Jonathan first appears in the Bible as the grandson of Moses; and curiously the initial appearance of names that include 'nachash'—or its variant 'nahas'—are Phinehas, grandson of Aaron, and Nachshon, the name of Aaron's brother-in-law. The cousins Phinehas and Jonathan are, as outlined in *God's Priority*, probably both named for Leviathan. They are a study in contrasts—one is on fire with zeal for God while the other commits an unspeakable atrocity. One is honourable; the other almost unimaginably dishonourable.

This sudden cluster of *monster* names given around the same time period might seem strange until we look at the description of Exodus in the Psalms.

> *You divided the sea by Your strength. You broke the heads of the sea monsters in the waters. You broke the heads of Leviathan in pieces. You gave him as food to people and desert creatures.*
>
> Psalm 74:13–14 NHEB

This provision must have been so amazing that people memorialised it in the names of their children. The crossing of the Red Sea was a threshold event; it was the moment of transition from slavery to freedom. And perhaps that fact has been telegraphed all along in the description of the sea as the 'Yam Suph' (which could mean *sea of reeds* but may also mean *sea of transition*, with additional overtones of *day of transition*).

Whenever Scripture describes threshold events, it signals them through certain markers. One such indication is the presence of angelic guardians—whether holy or unholy. During the Exodus, the Israelites were at one stage trapped between the armies of Pharaoh and the sea. The geography at that time is described in detail—and it alludes not just to difficult terrain but, as I've pointed out in *God's Pageantry*, to four different threshold guardians. The people of Israel were surrounded both physically and spiritually by hostile forces.

They were instructed (Exodus 14:2) to camp facing Pi-hahiroth. Apparently these were cliffs with sheer rock faces. *Strong's Lexicon* says Pi-hahiroth means *the place where sedge grows*, while *Cornwall & Smith* suggests *mouth of wrath* or *kindlings*. In other words, it's suggestive of Leviathan, the dragon with the flame-throwing mouth. This may seem subtle at first glance but when the other three names mentioned suggest Ziz, the spirit of forgetting, Python, the spirit of constriction and Rachab, the spirit of wasting, it's quite direct.[81]

Leviathan wants our inheritance—symbolised by land and a fruitful vineyard. It therefore wants to turn us back as soon as we've stepped into a space where our birthright will come to pass. There are certain things it can't take from us: salvation being one of them. But it can take our calling.

Because its natural home was originally the Inner Court of God, it's more likely to appear once we've actually passed over the threshold. On the threshold itself, we are likely to encounter the gatekeepers or door wardens—cherubim like Python or Rachab. Before we even get there we are likely to meet up with Ziz, the spirit of forgetting. Nonetheless, they can call for reinforcements if they feel under threat. And Leviathan is just one of several allies they can ask for assistance.

But back to what Leviathan wants: our inheritance. It wants to mark its ownership of our 'land' by putting its name on it. Now our 'land' may not be physical: it might be a business or a ministry that has very little material footprint, but a huge spiritual impact.

Nonetheless, we find Leviathan claiming possession of physical territory in quite recognisable ways.

For example, the City of London is the historic centre and local government district within the metropolis of Greater London. A business and financial hub with its own independent police force, it has a unique political status and a singular relationship with the Crown, such that even the reigning British monarch is formally required to stop at its borders and request entry. It has seven gates—though modern roads mute their existence. At ten locations, on its boundary, thirteen silver-and-red dragons stand guard.

These numbers are so reminiscent of the seven-headed dragon with ten horns mentioned in Revelation:

> *Then another sign appeared in heaven: a huge red dragon with seven heads, ten horns, and seven royal crowns on his heads.*
>
> Revelation 12:3 BSB

The name of London allegedly derives from Ludd, who supposedly founded a city on the banks of Thames in pre-Roman times. Ludd's background is a tangled thicket of English, Welsh, Norse and Celtic myth that's impossible to unravel. In addition there are plenty of evocative associations that relate on the one hand to water deities and on the other to multi-tailed comets—celestial objects that in many cultures are associated with dragons.

However bypassing all this and just looking at the word, Ludd, let's note that it was probably very close in pronunciation to 'Luth' or 'Lot'. The latter is a Biblical name associated with so much dishonour that we would struggle hard to find one in Scripture at a higher level.

Abraham's nephew Lot is named, in my view, for Lotan, the Canaanite equivalent of Leviathan. Lot had undoubtedly grown up immersed in pagan religion. After all, he was born about five hundred years *before* the Law was delivered at Sinai.

Now Lot is said to mean *wrapped* and Lotan *coiled* or *tightly wrapped*, while Leviathan is described as *twisted* or *coiled*. Both monsters are described in similar terms: 'fleeing serpent'[82] or 'fugitive serpent',[83] both 'wriggle' or 'twist',[84] both have multiple heads.[85]

Leviathan not only lashes its tail and spits fire, it also wraps itself in coils around its prey. This is the link between Lot, *covering*, Lotan, *tightly wrapped*, and Leviathan, *coiling serpent*.

In *God's Priority*, I've outlined the reasons why I think the disaster that overtakes Job parallels the tragedy of Lot and his family. In both stories, the fire of God fell from heaven—in the natural realm signifying a meteoric impact strike, in the spiritual indicating retaliation by Leviathan. Job's story shows that it's not necessary to be the perpetrator of dishonour to receive backlash: sometimes it's a simple matter of living in a defiling neighbourhood.

The same is not true for Lot, however. The first sign of dishonour in his story emerges when his herdsmen and those of Abraham[86] start quarrelling over grazing land. Both men became so rich in Egypt that the pasture was insufficient for their flocks. When conflict arose, Abraham suggested they move away from each other. He gave Lot first pick of the land.

Now Abraham had been a father figure to Lot.[87] The blessings God showered on Abraham were so lavish that Lot had benefited simply by being related to him. His wealth had clearly come to rival that of his uncle. For these reasons, Lot should have deferred to Abraham. But he lifted up his eyes and saw a landscape so lush it seemed comparable to the Garden of the Lord.

So Lot was drawn to a place that promised to be just like 'Eden': in the deepest of ironies it turned out to be Sodom, a city of the plain. It was a counterfeit of the first paradise: a spiritual equivalent of God's palatial royal court with its mountain, garden and four rivers. The new royal dwelling would be the Tabernacle with its Inner and Outer court and its Holy of Holies. Lot was lured to a fraudulent 'Inner Court' where dishonour and vice held sway.

In the true, legitimate Inner Court where the Levites minister, honour and righteousness abound. How did the Levites come to be gifted this office of a special priesthood? To begin with, all men had the right to be priests in their own household. Within a wider community, the firstborn son held the right to be priest for the family. But all this was lost when the men of Israel—and it's right to emphasise *men* here for many Jews hold the view that a close examination of the Hebrew text exonerates the women[88]—chose to worship the golden calf. Because the tribe of Levi responded to the call of Moses to come to God's side, they were recompensed with the right to be priests for the entire nation. Again we see honour bringing reward and dishonour drawing retaliation.

But back to Lot. When Sodom was attacked by a coalition of armies, he was taken captive. Abraham, learning of his plight, set out in pursuit and rescued him. This was a natural opportunity to break with the Corporation of the City of Sodom, but Lot didn't take it.

He went back to a society steeped in so much dishonour that God sent a pair of cherubim to investigate the outcry against it. These agents of judgment were throne guardians: that is, officers of God's court with plenipotentiary powers. This means their decisions were effectively those of God Himself.

When the residents of Sodom insisted that Lot send out his guests, this honourable man[89] was trapped in an invidious situation. He tried to uphold the threshold covenant with his guests and save them from dishonour by dishonouring his daughters instead. Whatever Lot's choice at this point, the consequences would be tragic.

Later, after the loss of his wife, Lot's daughters decided on a course of pre-meditated dishonour: they got their father drunk and became pregnant to him. They then named the children they conceived through incest so that his dishonour would be remembered in perpetuity. The tribes descending from Lot and his daughters are: Moab, *from my father*, and Ben-Ammi, *son of my father*. The land itself eventually came to be named after these ancestors of the Moabites and Ammonites. Again we have an encoding within the landscape itself of dishonour.

When the Israelites under the command of Joshua crossed the Jordan to take possession of the Promised Land, there were 31 kings, seven major cities and not a few giants to be overcome. There's a parallel between this inheritance and the Inner Court. The very first cities the Israelites conquered in Canaan demonstrate this correspondence.

There are two contenders for the meaning of the name, Jericho. One is *moon*[90] and the other is related to *nose* and *smell*—Jericho was renowned for its to-die-for perfumes in later ages. In fact, its modern Arabic name means *fragrant*.[91]

Each of us has a unique scent—as individual as fingerprints or retina markings. Isaiah suggests we will be judged, not by sight or sound, but by smell!

> *The Spirit of the Lord will rest on Him—the Spirit of wisdom and of understanding, the Spirit of counsel and of might, the Spirit of the knowledge and fear of the Lord—and He will delight in the fear of the Lord. He will*

> *not judge by what He sees with His eyes, or decide by what He hears with His ears but with righteousness.*
>
> Isaiah 11:2–4 NIV

The phrase '*delight in the fear*' also means '*understand the perfume*'. The sevenfold Spirit of God gives us to understand—discern—the fragrance of righteousness. Here we see why smell is the first and most significant of the senses to be conquered.

The second city conquered in the land was Ai, a name coming from the word for *eye*.

The twentieth city conquered was Lasharon, *tongue* or *tasty*, and the twenty-second was Hazor, a name related to the *sound of a trumpet* and to *the ear*.

Of the five natural senses of the body—sight, smell, taste, hearing and touch—the first four are referred to quite clearly. In addition, the sixth city, Lachish, denotes both *invincible* and an *obstinate* attitude. Perhaps this alludes to the missing sense of touch, since *obstinate* and *hard* are related in many cultures, including Hebrew.[92]

Furthermore there are other activities of the body: the seventeenth city, Tappuah derives from a word for *breath* and the ninth city Debir is about *words* or *speaking*.

The conquest of the Promised Land symbolises taming our own bodies. After coming into threshold covenant with God, our first acts should be about subduing our senses. Smell apparently isn't too hard at all—if we follow God's battle plan to lay siege to it. When we win back smell in the natural, we win discernment in the spiritual. And we need discernment—because the spiritual equivalent of the deceiving Gibeonites—won't take long to decide they want to covenant with us.

Listening and hearing are obviously a little harder—since they unite with other forces to try to repel our efforts. Just as the king of Hazor was the leader of a coalition of kingdoms against Joshua, so the spiritual 'ear'—when it doesn't want to hear—will muster an army as *'numerous as the sand on the seashore.'* (Joshua 11:4 NIV)

However, it's the battle to overcome the covetous nature of the 'eye' that brings us most trouble. We may have to apply our discernment from our victory over the nose in a serious effort to find our 'Achan'—the man of trouble[93] within ourselves determined to sabotage our achievements. This internal traitor continually invites trouble to follow us around, rather than goodness and mercy.

Now the correspondence between the landscape of ancient Israel and the human body has deeper implications. The Inner Court of the Tabernacle also has elements—the menorah, the altar of incense, the table of showbread—that correspond to the senses of sight, smell and taste, and that can be linked back to Leviathan.

But it is not Leviathan we are asked to make ourselves a dwelling place for: it is the Lord.

> *Do you not know that you are God's temple and that God's Spirit dwells in you?*
>
> 1 Corinthians 3:16 ESV

If we read this question in context, it's about the Day of the Lord and what will remain of our good works on that Day. Some of our efforts will be shown up as gold, silver and precious gems built on the foundation of Jesus Christ. Some will be revealed as nothing more than hay stubble and will be burnt up in the same fire that refines the gold. This passage is not about salvation—it's about sanctification. It's about our growth in holiness. It's about the privilege we are given us priests of the most High.

But when we dishonour anyone—anyone at all, even the satan himself—we bring down on our heads the legal right for Leviathan to retaliate. Dishonour is simply not compatible with peace, prosperity, health or wholeness—all those joyful aspects of shalom.

Holiness and honour are meant to hold hands. Together they enable us to don God's armour through receiving His kiss. As we stand to defend our inheritance, we won't be affected by the mesmerism of Leviathan attempting to enchant our sight so we are blinded to reality—seeing sin as beautiful and holiness as ugly.

Holiness and honour also help us sing over our inheritance. A fruitful vineyard is a symbol of inheritance in Scripture and God doesn't even ask us to guard and keep it. He once gave that duty to Adam but now He says He'll do it Himself. All He asks of us is to sing. Even though the terrible Day of the Lord has come:

> *In that Day,*
> *the Lord will punish with His sword—*
> *His fierce, great and powerful sword—*
> *Leviathan the gliding serpent,*
> *Leviathan the coiling serpent;*
> *He will slay the monster of the sea.*
> *In that Day—*
> *'Sing about a fruitful vineyard:*
> *I, the Lord, watch over it;*
> *I water it continually.*
> *I guard it day and night*
> *so that no one may harm it.'*
>
> Isaiah 27:1–3 NIV

Our inheritance is a gift of the Lord our Keeper. It is only as we stay close to Him; keeping short accounts with Him through repentance, forgiveness, renunciation and reconciliation that we receive back the stewardship of creation He always intended for us.

Rick and Patricia Ridings in *Shifting Nations Through Houses of Prayer*[94] speak of this vineyard song in Isaiah 27 and match it with another:

> *I will sing for the one I love a song about His vineyard: My loved one had a vineyard on a fertile hillside. He dug it up and cleared it of stones and planted it with the choicest vines. He built a watchtower in it.*
>
> Isaiah 5:1–2 NIV

They point out that these songs 'speak of anointed praise and worship as part of the spiritual covering of the vineyard we are given to watch over. They also allude to defending it from spiritual warfare.'

We're summoned to guard the vineyard of our inheritance—our calling—by praising God.[95] Because He inhabits the praises of His people, our acts of praise cause Him to dwell amongst us as our Keeper and covenant defender.

So when Leviathan makes its appearance within our inheritance—whether that's an actual geographical landscape; whether it's our calling, destiny and life purpose; whether it's our body—which could be the Body of Christ, the church, or alternatively our physical body—we should praise God. Because He will inhabit that praise and rebuke Leviathan for us.

Back at the beginning of the first chapter, I related my own encounter with Leviathan. 'Wow!' I said. 'One of God's great creatures! The one He made to frolic in the deep!' With those words I was praising God. It wasn't intentional, but no wonder Leviathan was taken aback. Although I wasn't aware of it, I was instinctively calling on God as my covenant defender.

Had I not done so, I would have been subject to Leviathan's occult specialty: enchantment. The Hebrew word 'nachash', *serpent*, is sometimes translated *divination* and sometimes *enchantment*. It derives from the word for *hiss* or *whisper*, and is a rhyme for a very similar word, 'lachash', *to whisper, beguile* or *charm*.[96] It also rhymes with 'rachash' which, amongst other things, means *creep like a reptile*.[97]

As mentioned previously, I believe Leviathan has a different expertise to other threshold guardians. Python specialises in *divination*, a counterfeit of prophecy in which words, signs and omens are analysed to foretell the future. This, at least to me, doesn't appear to be an activity associated with Leviathan.[98] On the other hand, *enchantment* does. There's a hint of that in the Garden of Eden where the fruit of the Tree of the Knowledge of Good and Evil appears triply desirable to Eve.

Were Adam and Eve enchanted? Mesmerised? Adam certainly acted very strangely. He was with Eve during the temptation[99] but he didn't correct her when she misquoted God, and added to His prohibition of not eating from the Tree that they were forbidden to touch it as well. Nor did Adam voice any doubts about the serpent's words, or suggest to Eve they should wait until after they'd checked with God to go ahead. He was silent throughout the entire exchange between his wife and the serpent.

Eve's was the first human sin of *com*mission; Adam's the first of *o*mission. Eve did something she shouldn't have done; Adam didn't do something he should have. He had been appointed the first 'shomer'—the guardian, the keeper, the protector. And he failed on his watch.

Whether he was enchanted or not—and I think there was a high probability he was—he was still held responsible by God. In fact, he was held to a higher accountability than Eve.

Enchantment is a theme running through much of the folklore about dragons. Looking into a dragon's eyes was always regarded as perilous because of the possibility of mesmerism, hypnotism or bedazzlement. There was always a risk of being beguiled and hoodwinked by the aura and glamour the dragon was able to cast.

But clearly we are not absolved of responsibility as a result. A friend testified about the insidious nature of enchantment and how it can become a false refuge—that is, a habit providing us with consolation and substituting for God in our lives. Here is Rosemary's story:

'For as long as I can remember I would say names over and over in my head. Anytime my mind was clear I would suddenly repeat a series of names over and over. Always those I was close to. Not always in the same order. In other times in my life it was different people close to me. I never really questioned why I did this, but I always remember doing it. I still don't know how or where in my life it started—maybe the Lord will reveal this or maybe He won't. Maybe I don't need to know how and why, only that my attention had been drawn to it recently as a problem.

A while ago I decided I needed to do something about it, so I determined that every time I started this in my mind I would turn it into prayer for these people directly. But this is such a strong habit that, in recent times, I often revert back to this repetitive naming. I asked the Lord directly about this and I do believe it is because of where I am with Him right now that He told me straight: *It is chanting. And not just chanting—EN-CHANTING.*

Like your twirling on the spot,[100] somewhere in my childhood/past I have taken to magic to help with my relationships. I would say it is very much to do with the spirit of

> rejection. I am still a bit in shock over this revelation. To think I was doing this really devastates me. How wonderful, patient, and merciful is our God!'

I can personally testify to that last statement. God is truly wonderful, patient and merciful! He knows that, in our century, we no longer know what magic is. I remember reading, many years ago now, a comment about the spiritual discernment of old countryfolk in Britain and Ireland at the end of the nineteenth century. It said, as I recall, they were aware the highest forms of black magic were virtually indistinguishable from prayer.

Until we recapture the reverential fear of God's holiness, the possibility we might be unknowingly practising the dark arts is going to escape us entirely. We become entrapped by our own ignorance. But ignorance is no excuse!

Leviathan wants to keep our vision captive and our minds spell-bound. Because then, even if we have crossed over the cornerstone and gone past the threshold guardians Python and Rachab, it's not going to help us hold on to the possession we've been granted. We won't see the subtle underminings occurring around us. We'll miss the 'the little foxes' digging their way into the vineyard.

> *Catch for us the foxes—the little foxes that ruin the vineyards—for our vineyards are in bloom.*
>
> Song of Solomon 2:15 BSB

Catching *'little foxes'* can refer to grabbing hold of temptations and turfing them out of our lives before they became messy, destructive habits. But little foxes can also be people influenced by unholy spirits; people sent to ruin our inheritance. Their assignment from Leviathan is to wreck as much as they can. At first, their actions are small and irritating but then they become increasingly more damaging. They act irrationally—and that's what catches us off guard as we try to reason with them. Their behaviour is both destructive and self-destructive—ultimately causing far greater harm to themselves than to us. You see, cultivated grapes—the kind you find in a vineyard—are fatal to foxes, just as they are poisonous to dogs.

When 'little foxes' in human form are sent against us, it's time to act decisively and promptly. Sing over the vineyard and ask the Lord our Keeper to rebuke Leviathan and to forbid backlash in the shape of 'little foxes'. For our own protection, as well as that of the 'little foxes' themselves, we have to be alert, watchful and awake. We can't afford for Leviathan to beguile or charm us and captivate our thoughts or hold our minds in thrall. When little foxes are unleashed against us, we have to catch them as soon as we notice them trying to dig their way in.

The fruit of shalom is lethal to Leviathan. That's why it will leave so swiftly when God's grace descends. Our blessing of peace has become its toxic payback for using fruit as a weapon in the conspiracy against mankind in

Eden. And the fruit in our vineyard is not just the grapes of shalom but a vine cluster of love, joy, peace, patience, kindness, goodness, faithfulness, gentleness and self-control.

Perhaps the most popular story in Scripture features David and Goliath. Brave, faith-filled kid defeats enemy giant with just a slingshot and some serious attitude. Let's unpack it so we can see the hidden influence of Leviathan on this famous episode.

Goliath means *splendour* and is generally thought to come from 'galah', *naked*.[101] Thus its root meaning would be *revealer of secrets* or *exposer of nakedness*. However, some lexicons list it as coming from 'galut', *exile*. These two ideas—*exile* and *nakedness*—are conceptually linked. If someone was exiled, they would be stripped of family, friends, the social benefits of community and the protection of the clan. Moreover, if they were *taken* into exile, as opposed to merely *sent*, they may well be stripped of clothes as well.

Now 'galut', more accurately, seems to be *unwrap* or *uncover*; related to 'lot', *wrapping* or *covering*. And as we've seen, 'lot' points directly to Leviathan through Lotan.

Goliath thus has the spirit of retaliation encoded in his name. For forty days, he tried to provoke the armies of Israel into battle—exposing the shallowness of Saul's faith in God as well as the fear dominating his forces. It's certainly an understandable fear: only Saul and Jonathan had armour so everyone else would have to go 'naked'—without body protection—into battle. But it wasn't really this self-evident nakedness Goliath exposed: it was the spiritual nakedness of a nation that had preferred a man as their king and not God. Ultimately, Goliath revealed the political nakedness of the Philistines as well. Their weakness was a military strategy entirely dependent on a single champion.

There are subtle ironies in the situation. Goliath, after all, is the one whose name comes from *naked*. However he is covered with bronze armour[102] while David has no protective covering. Except, of course, his faith in God.

As I've pointed out in *God's Poetry* and in *Name Covenants*, names encode both our identity and our calling. But this destiny cannot be found simply by looking at the *meaning* of any name: God, as a master poet, devises beautiful word-plays and clever puns in order to ensure that, whatever knowledge of our destiny the threshold spirits have and whatever snares they set as a consequence, it will never be enough to deny us our calling.

Now David, *beloved,* from 'dowd', rhymes with the Hebrew word for *exiled* or *wanderer* and sounds like words for *estranged, foreigner, enemy*.[103] These last words fittingly describe David's career as a mercenary commander allied with the Philistine king Achish. He was Achish's bodyguard.[104] And also Saul's armour-bearer.[105] In Israel, an armour-bearer routinely cut a covenant with his master and it's very likely this was also a Philistine practice. This would explain the unusual trust Achish put in David, a trust which horrified his Philistine compatriots since they rightly recognised the huge conflict of interest entailed.

So it transpires that David's conflict with Goliath, *the one who exiles*, is not simply a fight between national champions—it's also a clash of personal identities. Even in death—in fact, *because* of his death—Goliath managed to bring the *exile* of David to pass.[106] The rout of the Philistines by the victorious Israelites culminated in a song of celebration: '*Saul has slain his thousands and David his tens of thousands!*'[107]

Saul, on hearing the lyrics, flew into jealous rage. Eventually his obsession with killing his rival culminated in David's flight into exile and his alliance with the enemy.

Threaded through the entire episode is retaliation and dishonour. Goliath deliberately dishonoured the men of Israel, as well as Yahweh, in his twice-daily defiance. Saul had already displeased God on multiple occasions through disobedience—but, unlike David, he continually excused his own behaviour and did not repent of it. Eventually he reached a peak, not long before this encounter with Goliath, where his success in battle led him to dishonour God Himself.

> *Early in the morning Samuel got up and went to meet Saul, but he was told, 'Saul has gone to Carmel. There he has set up a monument in his own honour...'*
>
> 1 Samuel 15:12 NIV

When Samuel finally caught up with him, he started to make excuses for not obeying God's instructions in battle. Samuel cut him short and prophesied:

> *Rebellion is like the sin of divination, and arrogance is like the wickedness of idolatry. Because you have rejected the word of the Lord, He has rejected you as king.*
>
> 1 Samuel 15:23 BSB

Dishonour is the fruit of pride and arrogance. Saul's monument to himself is a symptom of that pride, which Samuel revealed as idolatry. It is no wonder that, when that pride was threatened by a song elevating David above himself, he first dishonoured David verbally, long before the physical attacks started.

It was all about retaliation. In fact, it was pre-emptive retaliation since Saul already sensed David as a threat to his throne.

Sometimes Leviathan can inspire pre-emptive retaliation in our lives. Usually all this does is cause a potential threat to become an actual threat. It's like a self-fulfilling prophecy—because when we dishonour others by pre-emptively retaliating we invite that same measure of reprisal—often multiplied many times over—upon our own heads.

Now I don't want to leave any discussion of Goliath and David without pointing out that the spiritual dynamic in operation is not solely the work of Leviathan. Python is also in evidence. In fact, the story of David and Goliath is prophetic of Jesus' encounter with Python: David's conquest of Goliath with a slingshot to the head links back to the divine prophecy, '*He will crush your head*,' and looks forward to Jesus' squashing Python's head.

Goliath was a descendent of the Nephilim through Anak, *the strangler*. The sons of Anak were the famous giants who intimidated the twelve spies sent to scout out the Promised Land. The Anakim were eventually expelled from Hebron by Caleb,[108] but obviously they then intermarried with the Philistines.

Anak's name reveals its affinity with the spirit of Python.[109] The *choker* or *strangler* lived up to its reputation when the twelve spies returned to Moses with a report that smothered any chance of the people agreeing to cross the threshold into the inheritance God had promised them.

That same choking was apparent when Saul and his armies faced Goliath. They'd taken on the Amalekites and beaten them hollow. They'd taken on the

Ammonites and trounced them. Jonathan had led them to victory against the Philistines, even in the middle of another bout of Saul's disobedience when his *worry*—our English word comes from the German *to strangle*—caused him to usurp the role of a high priest. Very much as we are apt to do so often when the worries of life consume us.

In all this, the most definitive sign of Python's presence in the situation of David and Goliath, though, is the jealousy of Saul. When Python is defeated—and clearly it was with Goliath's death—it will depart. But it will also leave behind a lingering defilement—the stench of jealousy. The temptation to react with envy is one we all have to fight as we watch others pass over their thresholds.

It's important to be aware of these different tactics of Python and Leviathan. Because a strategy that works to overcome one will not work for the other. Different fruit are needed in our weapon packs—*love*, agápē, to conquer Python and *peace*, shalom, to exile Leviathan.

The spirit behind Goliath hasn't left us; the display of dishonour he showed towards the people of Israel has not gone away, even in the twenty-first century. It's still rampant today amongst Christian believers. It's so common it even has a special designation: 'replacement theology'. This is the belief that the people of Israel have been replaced in God's purposes by the Christian church. Instead of being grafted in to God's covenant people and to the root stock of Israel, the church is said to have supplanted the descendents of Abraham. Allegedly, they have been cast aside by God. This is not only a failure to understand that the covenant of God with Abraham and all his generations is irrevocable; it is a failure to heed the warnings of Paul to those of us who are Gentiles, the wild olive branches of God's tree of healing for the nations:

> *If some of the branches have been broken off, and you, though a wild olive shoot, have been grafted in among the others and now share in the nourishing sap from the olive root, do not consider yourself to be superior to those other branches. If you do, consider this: You do not support the root, but the root supports you. You will say then, 'Branches were broken off so that I could be grafted in.' Granted. But they were broken off because of unbelief, and you stand by faith. Do not be arrogant, but tremble. For if God did not spare the natural branches, He will not spare you either.*
>
> Romans 11:17–21 NIV

When Scripture says, *'Honour everyone,'* God means it. When it says, *'Do not be arrogant, but tremble,'* God means it too. When it says, *'Do not consider yourself to be superior to those other branches,'* He means that as well.

Don't be haughty when it comes to the Jewish faith. Don't be conceited when it comes to other denominations. Don't mock politicians with insulting jokes. Don't call people 'Jezebel' or 'Ahab' or 'Daughter of Satan' or 'Son of Perdition'—leave such judgments to God.

> *'Vengeance is mine, and recompense.'*
>
> Deuteronomy 32:35 ESV

Do not put yourself in the talons of Leviathan. Simply honour everyone. And honour Jesus above all.

I shouldn't have to make that last remark. It should go without saying for Christians. But so often it doesn't. Quite a few people have elevated the writings of Paul above the words of Christ, giving the self-proclaimed 'least of the apostles' precedence—because he wrote from a post-resurrection perspective and Jesus spoke prior to the resurrection.

It's a lot like those Jews in the first century who believed Moses had dispensed manna from heaven, not God. Jesus shouldn't ever have had to say, *'Truly, truly, I tell you, it was not Moses who gave you the bread from heaven, but it is My Father who gives you the true bread from heaven.'* (John 6:32 BSB)

But deep in the human heart there's a bent towards elevating our culture heroes to god-like status. This tendency is called *euhemerism*. Basically a case of unbridled hero worship becomes so extreme that all flaws in the hero's character are overlooked. Such idols, by definition, can do no wrong. We enshrine them or enthrone them, allowing them to usurp the place of God in our lives.

Make no mistake about how common this is in today's world. I'm not talking here about believers who park their own views above the plain reading of Scripture and who have an evolutionary view of how humanity has understood God. They are simply crowning themselves. Installing yourself as king has happened since time immemorial.

No, I'm talking about believers who consider Paul to be the champion of the New Testament and who don't notice any faults in his behaviour after his conversion on the Damascus Road. I'm talking about believers who blindly accept the ancient view that God set Abraham ten tests and that he passed them all. I'm talking about believers who put a halo on Moses, who think David only fell once into sin, who consider that Ezra and Nehemiah were right in the way they acted to ensure racial purity.

I'm talking about idealised characters whose shortcomings are airbrushed out of sermons so that they become prototypes of perfection. Yet these romanticised visions have become the role models for today's aspiring platform-seekers.

I can't begin to describe my shock when I realised some theologians consider the words of Paul to be pre-eminent over the words of Jesus in any perceived conflict! I had suspected it for some time, actually thinking on numerous occasions to myself: 'This is written as if Paul is the hero of the New Testament, not Jesus.' But, unable to believe that anyone could ever think that way, I dismissed my own discernment.

Finally I realised I really had detected an attitude that was more prevalent than I could have ever dreamed possible. Within this theological stance, Paul ranks at the pinnacle of a hierarchy, Jesus next, John a bit further down, James possibly just scraping in at the ground floor while Peter and Jude are consigned to somewhere in the outer darkness.

This is theologically-sanctioned dishonour of God. It allows people to say, as has happened to me personally, 'We don't need to repent once we're saved. Paul doesn't speak of confessing sins in any of his epistles, so these things are unnecessary once we've accepted Christ as Lord.'[110]

This is not only dishonour of God, it's dishonour of Scripture. It alleges that John's message—*If we confess our sins to God, He can always be trusted to forgive us and take our sins away*[111]—is essentially meaningless. After all, it's not written to unbelievers but to those he says have *'faith in the son of God.'*[112]

We don't need to make Paul the alpha pack leader of the epistle-writing apostles. We don't need to ignore the flaws of our heroes either. Rather, we need to recognise that they, like us, need healing and that God loves us anyway. Let's realise that, although Absalom was exceedingly treacherous, he learned the art from his father. The reason Moses and Aaron were denied entry to the Promised Land was not because God was huffy that they'd struck the Rock,[113] it was because that action signified refusal of covenant. They had publicly announced to God, 'We don't want to cross the threshold into Your place.' That's exactly what striking a rock meant! Before God refused ever them, they'd refused God. They'd also dishonoured Him:

> *'Because you did not trust in Me enough to honour Me as holy in the sight of the Israelites, you will not bring this community into the land I give them.'*
>
> Numbers 20:12 NIV

God gave them just what they asked for. Sometimes a 'no' from heaven is not retaliation from Leviathan. Sometimes it's simply God giving us what we really asked for. Too late we realise our own folly, if we recognise it at all.

Let's learn to discern the difference.

Prayer

Abba Father, You have given me the vision of my personal Promised Land—Your special inheritance and chosen destiny for me. However I have failed to do what was necessary to pass over the threshold and into my calling. You gave me the vision and You gave me the choices but I turned to the easy option. I confess that I looked for convenience and safety, rather than Your will. It was not Your desire that I should choose second and even third best for my life. 'It is too hard' or 'I haven't the time' or 'Here I am, Lord—send someone else!' has been my repeated response.

I have come to a time in my life when I feel so unfulfilled and so empty, and wanting 'more' so very desperately. I finally realise the 'more' is You, Lord. I long to recapture Your vision for me. But I realise that my heart is conflicted. It wants You but it wants to hold on to the power and authority, the honour and respect, the gifts and talents, the accumulation of earthly treasure—all the things You've given me—and not surrender them to glorify You.

Lord, I come before You and I acknowledge that I failed to respect You and thank You for Your unshakable care and love for me. I admit that I failed to listen to You and respond to Your still quiet voice as You spoke in my mind and in my conscience. Father God, I am sorry. I am sorry I did not say, 'It *is* hard—but, with Your help, it is not *too* hard.' I am sorry I did not say, 'I *am* busy but You are my first priority for the day.' I am sorry I did not say, 'Here I am, Lord—send me.' I am sorry for the dishonour and disrespect that reigned in my life towards You. I am sorry I gave Leviathan such free access to my life. In Jesus' name, forgive me and set me free.

I hear Your voice saying, 'It's late but it's never too late. You are forgiven, beloved. Accept My forgiveness and, along with it, the freedom to make the needed choices to pass over the threshold and reach your Promised Land. Jesus has already said, "Yes," to your request and gives you the freedom to start again. Be blessed with singing as you go forward.'

Father, thank You for Your forgiveness, Your faithfulness, Your justice, Your mercy, Your lovingkindness and Your grace. I thank Jesus for being the all-sufficient sacrifice for my sin and for the right to enter my calling and receive my inheritance. I resolve, through the empowerment of Your grace and His blood, that from now on I will act with honour and respect to You and all Your creation in all areas of my life.

In the mighty name of Jesus and to His honour and glory. Amen.

7

Lines, Links, Land

20 March 2015
Tórshavn, Faroe Islands

IT WAS A COLD, OVERCAST MORNING. On the bare hillside around me were thousands of eager people, looking skywards, hoping against hope that the curtain of clouds would part and the celestial spectacle they'd come so far to see would appear. If you've never seen a total solar eclipse on the line of totality, it's impossible to imagine how wondrous it is.

Back in 2012, I'd persuaded my family to come on a holiday to see a total solar eclipse at Cairns in North Queensland. After it was over, one of my brothers said, 'You know, I wasn't actually expecting much. After all, *you* can get excited by just about anything astronomical. But I don't have words to describe something that beautiful. Where's the next one?'

It was in Somalia. We both immediately thought of pirates and decided to pass. And then this event in the Faroes, which had promised so much, was a damp and drizzly fizzer. All that could be seen of the eclipse from the vantage point were some indistinct reflections on the water. The weight of disappointment from the crowd was tangible.

The Faroe Islands, in the middle of the North Atlantic half-way between Scotland and Iceland, is a very long way to go to see nothing. And yet... and yet... I felt it was exactly what God wanted me to see. He'd sent me a message. All I had to do was translate it.

The first time I'd ever noticed a message in the landscape had been back in 2003. I'd been teaching in Alice Springs and, every weekend, I would head out on a tour to see more of Central Australia. One Saturday, it dawned on me as a tour bus rattled along a dusty back-road that it had been forty days since I arrived. 'Forty days in the desert!' I said to myself, thinking of how significant that time period is in so many Scriptural stories. I was in a heightened state of expectancy as the bus arrived at Rainbow Valley. We were there to see the sunset lights on the coloured rocks in an inverted bow of a hill. Until sundown, we had time to explore.

I set out along a sandy trail towards Mushroom Rock and, as I reached a corner, a surprise awaited. Right next to the trail was a rock shaped like a crouching lion and in the distance, in a vista opened up by the corner, was a cliff-face with the profile of a man. 'Rainbow, lion, man,' I thought. This was a time when I was very new to deciphering name covenants and really had very little idea what I was doing. But I had sufficient knowledge to be taken aback. *Rainbow*, *lion* and *man* would indicate the landscape was coded for someone named Lewis. I was relieved to realise that. Because *only* if there was a *tree* added to the symbolic equation would there be a message for a Hamilton.

Now I was aware of indigenous songlines. And I realised what I was sensing was both like and unlike them. Many believers simply think that, if there is any religious aspect at all to an aboriginal ceremony, it must have overtones straight from hell. Sometimes this is true as, for example, in Borneo where local Christians will warn you not to approach a spirit house because of the demons dancing on top of the incense.[114] The vast majority of westerners will consider this primitive superstition, but pause for a moment and consider what incense in God's temple is: the altar of incense symbolises the prayers and praise of the people of God rising to heaven. And if God inhabits the praise of His people, why wouldn't a counterfeit altar have something exactly similar—spirits dancing on the incense?

If there is a spiritual counterfeit, then the genuine counterpart must exist. In fact, I've often found a counterfeit first. I've even pondered the thought that Jesus must have been a stonemason, rather than a carpenter. The Greek word, 'tektón', used to describe

Him can mean either. But when was the last time you encountered a religious lodge with rites based on woodworking?

When it comes to lines in the landscape, I first realised their significance when talking with a friend who'd lived in Bali for many years. She often felt to pray regarding a particular volcano where she felt there'd been child sacrifice. She'd taken a photo of it once and when it was developed, more than a dozen tiny faces were evident in the picture. When she described this photo, it sounded mysterious but not too far-fetched. After all, the dappling of light and shadow on distant hills can often produce images that the human mind interprets as 'faces'. But then she showed me the photo! It was very old—from the days long before photoshop could alter images. And there in it were not vague blurry faces but astonishingly distinct and clearly identifiable features of Indonesian children.

My friend's ministry was singing praise to God on mountaintops. At one time, she'd managed to persuade a group of prominent pastors to come to Bali. One of them wanted to meet a local personality who was a Hindu priest and, since my friend knew him well, she arranged for them to spend an afternoon together. When that pastor came back from the meeting, he said, 'I have just met the greatest witchdoctor in the world.'

My friend, astonished, asked him how he'd arrived at that conclusion. It turned out the Hindu priest had been quite open about his own ministry. From time to time, as the goddess he served provided the funds, he would 'take' a mountain. He would travel to it, island-hopping across Indonesia and beyond, from one mountain to the next, opening a portal for the goddess through worship and prayer.

I was stunned as I heard this. My friend didn't seem to realise the implications of this disclosure. She hadn't seen that her own ministry was in direct opposition to that of this Hindu priest! She 'took' mountains by singing praise to God. He 'took' them by worshipping the goddess. It was no coincidence God had sent her to Bali to live.

As she told me about this priest attempting to ring the world by linking mountains in a line, I thought back to the trail I'd walked in Rainbow Valley. As soon as I reached Mushroom Rock, I knew my relief about the symbols in the landscape had been short-lived. Mushroom Rock was far more like a stone tree than it was like any fungus. So there was obviously a message in the landscape for someone named Hamilton. I figured that there were undoubtedly many people who shared my surname who had come that way but, most likely, none of them had retrieved the message waiting there. So it was up to me to do it.

These experiences—of picking up a message from God at Rainbow Valley and of hearing about a Hindu priest in Bali linking mountains—prepared me for watching an eclipse reflected by water. There had been an eerie silence on the hillside as the clouds maintained their vigil in front of the sun, blocking all but the indirect view of dappled light on the strangely still sea. Nothing like the excited hubbub of talk after the sunset eclipse at Lyndhurst in outback South Australia where the last glimpse of the returning sun had been a shark's tooth of light on the horizon. And nothing like the awed gasps as the clouds parted at Trinity Beach in Cairns, just as the bloom of light from the 'diamond ring' effect occurred. In the Faroe Islands, the silence of disappointment settled like a pall over the crowd.

Back in my cabin, later that day, I tried to come to grips with the deep impression I'd travelled halfway around the world to a non-event—but that I'd still seen precisely what God wanted me to see. I couldn't do justice to my feelings in words, so I tried to draw them. In fact, I tried to draw the three eclipses I'd seen in one picture: the eclipse at sunset, the eclipse at dawn and the eclipse reflected on the water. It needed perfect symmetry in my view because, after all, the calendar date was an equinox. Several attempts later I had my diagram. It seemed like something I should recognise—two pillars, one for sunrise, one for sundown, with waves between, and sun and moon above—but I was having difficulty translating it. I turned to my Bible and began looking for 'pillars of heaven'. I found the reference in Job:

> *He covers the face of the full moon and spreads over it His cloud. He has inscribed*

> *a circle on the face of the waters at the boundary between light and darkness. The pillars of heaven tremble and are astounded at His rebuke. By His power He stilled the sea; by His understanding He shattered Rahab. By His wind the heavens were made fair; His hand pierced the fleeing serpent.*
>
> Job 26:9–13 ESV

I read the first two verses twenty times—realising, in stunned disbelief, that they described an eclipse. 'Inscribing a circle on the face of the waters at the boundary between light and darkness' is a way of explaining the path of an eclipse. The one through the Faroes had followed a huge curve right up to the North Pole where it disappeared into space.

But the astonishing part of the verses was the flow-on connection to the sea monster Rachab[115] and to the fleeing serpent—which, since it is described as a 'nachash', I believe refers to Leviathan. I knew the ancient Chinese legend of an eclipse as a sun-eating dragon but hadn't connected it to Leviathan. In fact, for nearly three years after this, I thought this connection between an eclipse and Leviathan was a private revelation of the Holy Spirit—until the day I discovered one lexicon[116] actually suggests Job 3:8 (where a 'Day' is cursed and Leviathan is roused)[117] refers to an eclipse-causing dragon.

That day in the Faroe Islands I realised Leviathan uses lines on the earth's surface to come and go—particularly to flee when it senses trouble. The kind of trouble that occurs when believers, acting in honour under our high priest Jesus, begin to fructify with *shalom*.

The woman who'd emailed me from a tiny town on the east coast of New Zealand about the retaliation she'd been subjected to all her life had started a chain reaction. When we uncovered the rousing of Leviathan on the day she was born, I asked her if there was anyone in her home town who could pray into this specific matter for her. Not just pray *for* her; but pray *into* the matter leading her through all the forgiveness and even repentance that was necessary.

'Yes!' she said and went to see the local Anglican minister and his wife.

Several months later I was speaking at a seminar in New Zealand when I realised the minister and his wife were present. I dashed up to them, thanked them for their help, and then hurried to the podium. That was that.

Or so I thought. But the chain reaction was about to reach critical mass. Shortly afterwards a message popped up in my emails from the minister's wife. I recognised Joy's name, even though our acquaintance was limited to that brief 'hello-thanks-bye' at the seminar.

As I was about to open the message, I felt a quickening of the Holy Spirit. '*This message,*' He said, '*is about the prophecy your father made the day before he died.*'

I freaked out. And didn't open Joy's message for two days. I was intensely afraid I really had heard from the Holy Spirit but I was equally afraid I hadn't. It was an 'I-can't-move' moment, though of a radically different kind.

My dad had passed away in January 2009. The day before he died, as he was in a semi-conscious state, he garbled a lot in a morphine-induced rave. But as I listened, I was struck by a sudden realisation: actually it wasn't mindless babbling. He was speaking out a prophecy.

I quickly scribbled it down. It was about hospitals of the Holy Spirit for healing of the soul, in tiny towns along the east coast of New Zealand. It included a list of things needed to set them up.

At the time, I was puzzled. My dad had been a chairman of a healing ministry until he'd got cancer—so it was natural he'd think about 'Holy Spirit hospitals'. But— he was an Australian! He'd visited New Zealand very briefly just a few times in his life, mostly to look at engineering projects. It seemed exceptionally odd that his mind should turn to another country at such a crucial time and not to his own nation where he'd laboured to advance the Kingdom of God for so long.

After he died, I kept the notes of the prophecy carefully for a while. But as the years went by and life chugged on, I lost them. Even the memory of their existence faded until that day in early 2018 when Joy's unexpected message arrived in my inbox.

Her email was about the struggle of trying to minister in a small town with a dwindling congregation. She acknowledged she was close to despair regarding her heart's desire: a 'hospital of the Holy Spirit' for the healing of souls in her church.

As I saw the words, *hospital of the Holy Spirit*, my heart frisked. Yes, I had heard from the Holy Spirit. Yes, my dad had spoken a prophecy. Yes, it was clear I was called to help Joy and her husband achieve this.

But how?

None of us had a clue. But, as I listened to Joy's story and read her account of what the Lord had called her to do in the previous few years, I realised that—like the woman in Bali whose ministry was in direct opposition to that of the local Hindu priest—she was called to spiritually oppose a well-known national identity. And I realised Leviathan was working overtime in her town.

Over the next few years, I visited Joy and Richard several times—getting a feel for the landscape and what was encoded in it. I was looking for the messages like the one at Rainbow Valley that the Lord had hidden in plain sight. On the first visit, two important clues came to light. One came as a result of visiting the local museum. It had a video presentation on a local island explaining its history and the legends associated with it. Maui, the demi-god who is said to have dredged up a stingray from the seabed to form the North Island of New Zealand, baited the barb of his hook with his own blood. That barb, broken off, is said to be an island just off the coast.[118]

Now, by my reckoning, the use of blood indicated a covenant. And, assuming this reckoning was correct, then this was a counterfeit of the blood covenant God made with Abram. Therefore a 'torch' and an 'oven' (or 'smoking pot') should be present, just as in Abram's story. The 'torch' was obvious. It was a lighthouse—moved to the mainland and just a few hundred metres away from the museum. The 'oven' didn't become apparent until my third trip—when it became evident it was symbolised by an old whaler's boiling pot. We'd been looking diligently for the 'oven' anywhere within thirty kilometres, but it turned up right next to the lighthouse!

The second important clue had actually been told to me at a conference the previous year. Someone had informed me that God told them to tell me that the name of the angel of East Cape was 'Equation'. I wasn't ever sure I'd be able to use this information but I kept it in the back of my mind. I also kept in mind that an equation isn't especially useful unless you substitute into the formula to find the answer. But I didn't know what the formula was or what to substitute.

However, on this first visit, I began to suspect the name 'Equation' was in itself the formula and the substitutions were not numbers but words. Was it 'equus' for *horse* instead of *equal*? But what would work for the 'tion' or was it 'shun'?

On the second occasion I visited, Joy, Richard and I went travelling with a group of Aussies around East Cape. Singing praises to God as we went, it was a journey of great revelation. It was at Opotiki the jigsaw pieces started to come together. The first New Zealand martyr was gruesomely murdered at Opotiki inside a church originally called 'Zion'.

Could the correct substitution for the last syllable of 'Equation' be actually be *Zion*? More than one Māori iwi claimed that *their* mountain—the one from which they drew their tribal identity—was the true Zion. Theirs was the mountain Jesus would ride down on His white horse when He returned at the end of the age.

The carvings in the town centre at Opotiki were—hopefully unintentionally—reminiscent of the hideous murder of the first national martyr. Then, like scales falling off my eyes, I saw the name of the town differently: optik. The issue was *vision*. The land had been robbed of vision. And it had been robbed of it by layer upon layer upon layer of dishonour.

Later, during a worship time at East Cape, two horses came up as the singing began—one white and one brown—walking together, symbolic of Pakeha and Maori. *Horses of Zion*, I thought—not as a *replacement* for Zion in Israel but as a *complement*.

On my third visit, I met a man named Sam. 'Where do you get your power?' Sam wanted to know.

What sort of question is that? I wondered how Sam could not know about the Holy Spirit, given we were at a Christian conference. I'd spoken during the time about Zion and the longing, hidden within the heart of many New Zealand Christians, to usurp the place of the firstborn—as if their own national identity were not enough. It is deep within many cultures—not just New Zealand—part of it built on the British yearning to take that bow of burning gold, the arrows of desire, the spear and chariot of fire, and to build Jerusalem in England's green and pleasant land.

I apologise to my Kiwi friends for using your nation as an example. Because this is definitely not limited to Aotearoa. It's a worldwide problem—remember Dennis Conner's statement, 'We cannot lose. God is an American'? And perhaps you're aware that in Denmark, a revised Bible translation has removed the word 'Israel' in the New Testament and generally replaced it with references to the church.[119]

A programme of city beautification was undertaken at the end of the last century by the Christchurch City Council in preparation for the return of Jesus—who was expected to ride His chariot into town, just as the new millennium began! All but one of those projects was subsequently destroyed in the earthquakes of 2011.

Back around 1833, Penetana Papahurihia[120] claimed the *nachash* of Genesis 3 visited him. The *first* Māori prophet[121] to combine Christianity with Māori beliefs, he systemised teaching called *Te Nakahi*, Māori for *nachash*. He allegedly taught his followers they were Hurai—the people of Israel.[122]

Like the actions of the Christchurch City Council, this is a form of replacement theology: it says the promises of God to the people of Israel no longer apply to the Jews, but solely to Christians. This desire to be the firstborn dishonours not only the Jewish people but God Himself. If we say God is not going to meet any of His as-yet unfulfilled promises to Israel, we are calling His Word into disrepute. We are dishonouring Him and giving legal ground to the enemy.

The Gentiles are grafted in to the Vine; they are not a substitute for the root stock. When we say otherwise, we're telling God we're dissatisfied with who He made us to be. As if being anything other than a Jew is to somehow be sub-standard. To be inferior. As if it is not the highest honour to be a citizen of the nation to which God has assigned us.

How has Leviathan used this dishonour around the world? To judge by what's happened in New Zealand:

loss of vision, loss of discernment, loss of appetite for the things of God. Everywhere. And, as Scripture says, without vision the people perish.

Sam wanted to know how I'd seen so much. In his view, I should have been totally blind to the clues in the landscape. What were the Watchers doing that they didn't notice I'd seen right through them? How could someone from another country see what the locals couldn't? I finally realised Sam wanted to know what tattoo I had. His tattoo, he revealed, gave him the power to see into his neighbour's house and what his kids were doing back home when he was out. This was a really significant piece of information—because it told me what occult power the 'genius loci', *the spirit of the place*, offered those who wore its mark. It gave far-seeing and x-ray vision to its devotees; it also blinded outsiders. This is the case for all tribal tattoos—though different designs give different powers, depending on the tutelary spirit.[123]

As I was about to visit this tiny town for the third time, God directed my attention several times to Psalm 82. In fact, I was sitting in the airport lounge at Gate 82, checking the Hebrew of the psalm, when I realised there was a word in the opening line with a double meaning.

> *God has taken His place in the divine council;*
> *in the midst of the gods He holds judgment.*
>
> Psalm 82:1 ESV

This is a prophecy about Jesus going to the high mountain where the godlings of the nations held their assembly: He did this at the Transfiguration. He marched in on the *'sons of pride'*, the *'young lions'* Leviathan rules over, and effectively declared their sovereignty was at an end. Then, on coming down the mountain, He appointed His own government of seventy disciples and He sent them out to proclaim the coming of the Kingdom in the small villages of a foreign country.

Uh oh, I thought, as I looked at that Hebrew text. *I'm going to a small village in a foreign country and I've just realised the word translated 'in the midst of' is also the word for 'war'*. Jesus was interrupting a war council! *Which means I'm going to a war.*

'Can I go home?' I asked God.

'Your bag is already on the plane,' He said.

Deep sigh. 'You've got a really good strategy, don't You? Because You know how much I hate war.'

'A strategy over four decades in the making.'

Four decades. I was able to be a catalyst for some of the last steps the spiritual leaders in this town needed to make to overcome Leviathan. And, as I look back, I recognise many faithful people were involved over those forty years. I got to be in at the 'kill' yet many believers did the hard yards in preparing the way.

Leviathan fears being pierced. Scripture prophesies that will happen by the Lord Himself so, if there is any likelihood we are about to call on the Lord as the 'Man of War', it flees—wriggling, twisting and coiling away along lines it has created in the landscape. These escape routes join points it has marked out for itself in various localities. Some people call these channels 'ley lines'; others relate them to 'feng shui'; a slightly more scientific-sounding name is geomancy. In effect, it's divination involving the earth itself.

Lines can be created naturally, as in the shadows of eclipses. Or artificially: occult practitioners can create focal points to channel energy along the lines and into the hubs Leviathan uses for its own purposes.

What I realised about this tiny town was this: Leviathan had marked the place for its own through the legends of the guardian taniwha as well as ancient covenants. It had created an entire hub of lines in and out—very much, I believe, to take possession in the same sort of way that God had given Joshua every place where he placed his foot.

However God had put together a body of people—many unknown to each other—who, over four decades, had cut every escape route it had. God's long-term strategy was to trap it. And then bring to town a very knowledgeable person who knew exactly what needed to be done in terms of reconciliation, repentance and forgiveness before it could be pierced. And that very knowledgeable person was definitely not me!

It has to be a Body of believers to overcome the spirit of Leviathan. The genuine fluid Joining of God's people with Christ at the head has to confront the stiff counterfeit Joints riveted together by the dragon with the seven crowned heads. One amazing aspect of my experience in New Zealand was the way people looked at others they'd known for years, suddenly realising those they'd dismissed as a complete zero in the spiritual gift department had been quietly bringing down massive strongholds. They began to respect and honour each other!

Leviathan wants to be all-in-all: it's a counterfeit of both the Body of Christ and of Jesus, as a priest after the order of Melchizedek—king of Salem, the city of *shalom*. Thus the genuine Body of Christ under Jesus, our Head, has to use the fruit of *shalom* to overcome it.

We can't go up against Leviathan as individuals. That's a terrible mistake. Because it involves elitism and pride, not *shalom*. We can't even do it as a small group, or as a single denomination. That's a terrible mistake. Because it involves elitism and pride, not *shalom*.

This involves waiting on God. Waiting, as Joy found, to the very edge of despair. In Hebrew, *waiting* is the same word as *binding*. In fact, it's binding by twisting together. The twist that Leviathan counterfeits and wants to flick aside is our intimate expectancy of God's love in making over an inheritance in our name. We're not called to bind Leviathan, to wait on him and so deliver our inheritance into its claws—but rather to wait on God, anticipating the coming of His shalom.

It's not the end of the story for this little town because, when Leviathan is defeated, it's apt to call up its allies—Ziz, spirit of forgetting, and Lilith, a vampire spirit. Unlike Leviathan, Lilith doesn't fear piercing. But, like Leviathan, it is subject to rebuke from God.

> *But even Michael, one of the mightiest of the angels, did not dare accuse the devil of blasphemy, but simply said, 'The Lord rebuke you!'*
>
> Jude 1:9 NLT

Don't rush in where angels fear to tread! Instead rely on our covenant defender to do what He does best: kiss us with His armour.

> *I have given you every place where the sole of your foot will tread, just as I promised to Moses.*
>
> Joshua 1:3 BSB

This was God's pledge to Joshua. And it found its ultimate fulfilment in the second Joshua—Jesus of Nazareth. Whatever place Jesus put His foot was given to Him. Yes, there were exceptions—His hometown, Capernaum, Chorazin. But as a general rule, wherever He walked, healing flowed in the wake of His footsteps across long-defiled landscapes.

In the Samaritan town of Sychar, He healed the rift brought about by the edict of a king's cupbearer by asking a woman to be His cupbearer. All He did as an opening gambit was say: 'Give Me a drink.' He also re-unified the kingdom of David in the process.

In the land of the Gadarenes—the region just behind the heavily fortified eastern frontier of the Roman Empire and the ancient homeland of the tribe of Gad, *a troop*—He healed a man possessed by Legion. It wasn't just about the man, it was about the land and the trauma it suffered.

At Jericho, a town rebuilt at the cost of a firstborn son for the foundation and the youngest son for the gates, He healed two men: blind Bartimaeus, a name meaning *son of the foundation*, and Zacchaeus who climbed a sycamore tree so he could look down from on high and see Jesus. Segub, the youngest son whose life was the price of the gates of Jericho, means *on high*. The healings were pivotal because they weren't just about people, they were about history.[124]

Wherever Jesus went, His healings had this sparkling, diamond-edged aspect that few people notice: His work of mending the past was so subtle it is almost invisible.

Yet He was invariably erasing the peculiar stain of defilement unique to each locality. He was walking the land, and with each step of His foot, unpicking the lines that Leviathan had set up and that were criss-crossing the landscape.

When Jesus was dying on the cross, there was an impossible eclipse.[125] Impossible because it was the Passover and therefore full moon—thus it could not have been a solar eclipse. Yet it was daytime, so it cannot have been a lunar eclipse either. Now both Leviathan and Ziz are associated with eclipses. But neither of them can claim creation of that peculiar darkness from noon to three on the afternoon before the Passover. Nor do we have to scratch around for a scientific explanation. We won't find one. Because this is the 'strange work', the 'disturbing task', the 'alien act', the 'mysterious deed' that occurs in the natural world when God annuls a covenant with Death. Normally a covenant is forever, following family lines in perpetuity. Yet, in Isaiah 28: 21, God Himself pledged to cancel the perverse bargain people strike with Death in exchange for survival.

People can lose their faith so catastrophically that they come to believe God is not the most powerful being in the universe. Instead, they decide Death is. And they covenant with it for protection against itself—just as business owners bribe protection rackets. Such a covenant forfeits their own calling, the destiny of their children and any possible inheritance their descendants might have received.

A covenant is the strongest of all possible legal impediments to entering our spiritual calling—whether it's a covenant with Death, a covenant with Leviathan, a covenant with any of the threshold spirits.[126]

Yet God has promised to restore what has been stolen, to terminate the legal rights of the enemy, to take us back to Himself. Jesus triumphed over Leviathan at the cross. Still there's a sense in which the fulfilment of His work is yet to be. That's not to say He didn't finish what He set out to accomplish—but rather that, like many attainments, it is both once and future, both now and not-yet, both past and still to come. He is our priest and our pattern, perfectly fulfilling prophecy while at the same time also foreshadowing events belonging to our own era and beyond.

Perhaps Leviathan is the seven-headed dragon of Revelation with ten horns and seven crowns. Many people think so. This red dragon is clearly identified with the satan. So it should be a simple equation: the satan equals the dragon equals Leviathan. But this logic of positively identifying Leviathan as the satan only works if there's just one dragon.

Personally I think Rachab is also a dragon. And perhaps others of the fallen threshold guardians can also be classified that way. I suspect that 'the satan' refers to any member of this conspiracy of seven spirits who are all adversaries of mankind. After all, it's not as if there's only one seven-headed entity—to complicate matters, there's the seven-headed Beast who is given power by the Dragon. And then there's a second Beast who exercises all the authority of the first Beast.

But, at the end of the Day, it's never about the enemies of God. Yes, we need not to be ignorant of their schemes—but so we don't fall into the traps that have snared us before. We need to keep our eyes on Jesus.

When He came to earth, He emptied Himself. He died on the cross, taking the dishonour and shame that was our rightful portion, so that honour and glory might be returned to us. That we in turn may offer honour, like fragrant incense, before the throne of God.

Let us not fling the gift of Jesus back at Him through the stench of dishonour. Instead let us ask Him to plant seeds of shalom in our lives, so that when they blossom and flower, we can spread the aroma of Him wherever we go. And when they mature into plump fruit, we can place them as fine wine or heaped bowls on that table in the presence of our enemies—the spirits of the threshold—and distribute them to all the Lord invites to the feast with Him and ourselves.

Prayer for the Land

A reminder: read the prayer through carefully *before* saying aloud with intentionality. If you feel a check in your spirit from the Holy Spirit about any aspect of it, then heed the prompt. Put off praying until you receive permission. Don't dishonour God through presumption. **This is not a prayer for individuals; it is corporate in nature.** Be mindful that Leviathan is a *joined* entity, counterfeiting the Body of Christ and the priesthood of believers. So the Body of Christ, under the command and timing of Jesus our Head, needs to move in unity against it—not individuals or even small groups.

Lord Jesus, we know You are Immanuel, *God with us*, so You are with us.

Yet we ask You to come as our mediator and paraclete in a special way, to walk the land with us and in us. We ask You to place Your pierced and wounded feet wherever we step. We ask You to write Your name along the lines and over the land Leviathan has claimed for its own. We ask You, the pierced One, to pierce our enemy with shalom. We ask You, as our 'shomer', our watchman-guardian and kinsman-redeemer, to protect the land our feet have trodden and that our eyes have looked upon. We ask You to bless the people who dwell on this land, gifting them with refreshment and recompense, restitution and revival.

Lord Jesus, we ask You to bring simple healings—washings and cleansings—to the land. We ask You too to bring complex healings—purifications and anointings—to the land. We ask You to lift off all the layered wrappings of dishonour and disgrace, the deathly stench of defilement and resentment, and the warping and disfigurement caused by ancient vengeance. We ask You also to answer the cry for justice of the blood still calling from the land with Your own blood—the blood of the Lamb slain before the foundation of the world. We ask You to sing over the land and to mend it, so it is ready to gift as an inheritance to Your bride.

Father, we ask You too to sing over it with Your Son. Lead us in Your song, sing together over us, teach us to harmonise with Your song. May we join in with Your Body, under our Head—the Lord Jesus Christ—so that together with Him and the Holy Spirit, we will raise a never-ending symphony of praise to Your name.

Blessing and honour and glory and power, be to the One who sits on the Throne and to the Lamb forever and ever. Amen.

... to be continued

in

Dealing with Resheph:

Spirit of Trouble
Strategies for the Threshold #6

Appendix 1

Summary

LEVIATHAN IS A MONSTER of the deep, an angelic power, a sacred space, a map of the holy, a governmental system, a protector of honour, a counterfeit of the Body of Christ, king over the sons of pride and ruler over the 'young lions'—the principalities of the nations.

Its name means *wreathed* or *crowned*, or *joined sea monster* or *coiling dragon*. Leviathan twists communication and distorts the meaning of words. It may be the red dragon of Revelation. It may also be the serpent of Eden. Another name for Leviathan may be Resheph.

We sense its presence when we describe our situation as involving retribution, payback, backlash, blowback, kickback, whiplash, repercussions, reprisal or revenge. Its symbol is the crocodile, scorpion or anything with lashing tail, such as a stingray. It may also be imaged as a dragon, whale, hydra, manticore or basilisk. Actions indicating its presence are flame-throwing, acid-flicking, incense-burning or a 'death roll'.

Its occult speciality is enchantment, that is, mesmerism, hypnotism or the casting of a glamour.

God made it to frolic in the deep. It is fearsome and majestic and its Creator tells us that if we lay hand on it, we will remember the battle and never do it again. It is a multi-headed serpent and, because it is equivalent to the Canaanite chaos monster Lotan and also because of its connection with the menorah, the number of heads appears to be seven. This then further links it with the seven-headed naga of Angkor Wat, as well as the seven-headed serpent of Sumerian mythology who was slain and placed over a shining cross-beam of a chariot. As a dragon, it has links in the landscape to China and other Asian countries; to England and Wales, in particular the City of London with its gate guardians; to the taniwha of New Zealand; to the rainbow serpent of Australia and of Central America.

Its connection with rivers links it to the Nile in Egypt, to the Litani in Lebanon, to the Yangtze and Yellow Rivers in China as well as many smaller streams around the world which have dragon legends associated with them. In short, Leviathan is associated with features in the landscape and tries to create lines and hub points to facilitate its movement. These territorial markings counterfeit God's placement of His name on the land of Israel, as well as the positioning of the Levites within the land to unite the people by their presence and priestly ministry. The lines in the landscape make claims on the countryside, similar to the right that God gave to Joshua to possess every place where the sole of his foot trod.

It is a 'nachash', that is, a *fire-serpent*, like the six-winged seraph—the only angelic beings described as having wings. The function of the priestly Levites in the Inner Court of the Tabernacle and Temple mirrors the original purpose of Leviathan within the heavenly courts. Because the offices of God are irrevocable then, even as a fallen seraph, Leviathan is able to discharge its duty to ensure the court is a place of honour and holiness. It is savage in its reprisal against dishonour. Its legal rights can be removed through repentance, forgiveness and renunciation of covenant. All these need empowerment by the blood of Jesus.

It fears being pierced. The Fruit of the Spirit, *shalom* or peace, overcomes it.

Its description corresponds to the furniture of the Inner Court: seven heads like the seven-branched menorah; food like the Bread of the Presence; fire and smoke like the incense altar. It affects our vision, discernment, appetite, and connectivity. It wants to blind us spiritually, rob us of wisdom, make the Word of God tasteless and isolate us.

Jesus has given us many examples of healing the land from the effects of Leviathan and thus provided us with general guidelines to follow. Biblical stories, with the exception of Job, are generally very subtle in the way they show the involvement of Leviathan. Such stories include Lot and his daughters; the temptation of Adam and Eve; the landscape of the Exodus; David and Goliath; David and Ahithophel; David, Rizpah and the breaking of the famine; Elijah and the widow of Zarephath; King Uzziah in the Temple.

Appendix 2

Honour and Dishonour

Dishonour of God today:

IN TODAY'S CHRISTIAN WORLD, many believers have a tendency to unknowingly dishonour God. More recent variations on this theme are:

- attempting to use the blood of Jesus to cover actions that violate the Word of God, such as cursing others

- using the courts of heaven on the basis of personal need, rather than of prophetic calling

- appropriating the tools of spiritual healing to fix the mess we're in, rather than the mess we are

- declarations of binding and loosing, without repenting or forgiving

It's all about bypassing grace as the power to overcome sin. We don't want to overcome sin, we simply want to avoid the consequences. Thus God's grace is regarded as His 'forgetting' our sin because of the shed Blood of Jesus, rather than as the power that operates through that Blood to enable us to conquer sin.

Dishonour of Jesus today:

- Considering the words of Paul in the epistles to take precedence over the words and actions of Jesus. Because Paul is post-resurrection and the words of Jesus occur before the resurrection!

- Inappropriate burden-bearing to the point where we take on the sins of others: sin-eating and disease-eating where we become the 'saviour' and accept the retaliation others are due to reap.

- Making up fake testimonies about healings, miracles, angelic protection, visions and dreams. This calls the genuine stories into disrepute, suggests God needs our help to glorify His name, and makes the Truth into a lie.

- Believing in 'justification by doctrine' but calling it 'justification by faith'. Believing we are saved by faith, not by grace through faith; thus subtly adding our own efforts to the work of Jesus.

- Using the authority Jesus has given us, not to uphold the will and the word of God, but to bypass it.

Dishonour of the Holy Spirit today:

- Revelation without repentance, reconciliation or righteousness: using the gift of prophecy to promote the prophet, rather than God. Prophetic revelation may be given for the purposes of private intercession, rather than public utterance, and is simply part of God's counsel.

- Revelation without corroboration, verification, authentication, reconstruction, recognition or refinement. Ignoring the Scriptural requirement for the confirming testimony of two or three independent witnesses.

- Assessing other believers by their gifts, not their fruit; despite the words of Jesus that we are to know others by their fruit. Also despite the fact the gifts and offices of God are irrevocable and are no indication of character.

Honour everyone.

Let's spell this out because it seems to be so readily misunderstood.

- Honour your father and mother so that things will go well with you.
    - But do not honour them more than you honour God.

- Honour your wife so that your prayers will not be hindered.
    - But do not idolise her. The same applies to a wife: honour your husband but do not idolise him.

- Honour your children and do not exasperate them.
    - But do not honour your children more than you honour God or the curse of the House of Eli might follow your bloodline.

- Honour the government. Honour the authorities placed over you. Honour your leaders—even those who are deceased.
    - Your land will suffer if you dishonour the governing authorities. Do not think that, to honour those in authority, you must place them above correction. That position belongs to God alone. It is dishonour to always affirm without ever pointing out wrong-doing.

- Honour those you serve or those you employ.
    - Do not honour only those who can benefit you or those who are higher than you. Honour is meant to be mutual—*not* one-sided or one-directional. Nor is it meant to protective of institutions at the expense of the individuals the institution is supposed to serve.

- Honour the prophets.
    - You will receive a prophet's reward. But don't turn off your own gift of discernment when it

comes to assessing their words or the timing of their words. A true revelation given out of season may do more harm than good, by alerting the enemy to God's future plans.

- Honour the people of God, including the people of Israel. God chose the descendents of Abraham and promised them an everlasting covenant. Jesus was, and is, a Jew.

    o Do not subscribe to replacement theology. The Gentiles are grafted into the people of God, they are **not** substitutes for them. Do not flirt with anti-Semitic views.

- Honour people of other races, political views and religious persuasions.

    o But don't allow them to defile your spaces. Disagree agreeably. Do not become complicit with the media when it dishonours anyone.

- Honour the Lord's Supper.

    o If you do not discern the Lord in the bread and the cup, you eat and drink your own condemnation. Sickness, even death, is a direct consequence of dishonouring Jesus in this fashion. (1 Corinthians 11:29–30)

- Honour the Scriptures.
    - Don't create a hierarchy of any kind: whether that's thinking Paul's epistles are superior to the words of Jesus or that the New Testament supersedes the Hebrew writings. Yet the books of the 'Old Testament' are the only Scriptures Jesus used; they are the Scriptures the Bereans searched when they honorably examined what Paul preached; they are the Scriptures Paul was referring to when he told Timothy *'all Scripture is breathed out by God and profitable for teaching, for reproof, for correction, and for training in righteousness.'* (2 Timothy 3:16 ESV)

- Honour God's plan and purposes.
    - Don't honour your own way of thinking more than God's way. Don't enthrone logic. Don't enthrone intuition either. Don't ask the Lord of Hosts to sacrifice His battleplan because you have come up with a better strategy for your life.

- Honour your word.
    - Let your *yes* be **yes**, and your *no* be **no**.

- Honour the calling God has given you to steward.
    - But do not honour your own position or gifting more than you honour God. Do not

allow others to honour you or your advice more than they honour God. Do not become addicted to the honour because you will be unable to step down off the pedestal.

- Honour yourself.
    - But don't make an idol of honour. Don't honour Honour more than you honour God. Don't honour others more than God. Don't honour yourself more than God. But don't not honour yourself either. This is particularly difficult sometimes in abuse situations. Where the church has emphasised forgiveness by the abused but not coupled this with an equal emphasis on repentance by the abuser, honour is denied. Such dishonour opens the door for the spirit of Belial and, when it is involved, the Lord allows us to separate without attempting reconciliation. (2 Corinthians 6:15–17)

    - Don't gossip. Don't provide Leviathan with the opportunity to twist your words into slander. Don't copy the very activity that resulted in the expulsion of the satan from heaven—*trading*, with the implication that this trading involved names and reputation, calling and destiny, and ultimately honour.

- Honour your conscience.
    - If you don't obey your conscience, you are dishonouring the voice of God. Your conscience may in fact be wrong, but that's irrelevant. This is one of the principles behind Paul's instruction in 1 Corinthians 8:9–13.
- Honour creation and the spirit realm.
    - When it comes to fallen angels, don't dishonour them. Keep your focus on God and ask Him to rebuke them for you. If you engage them directly, you can expect retaliation. It's wise to repent of pride.

And lastly:

HONOUR GOD ABOVE ALL.

Appendix 3

Honouring Others

SO WHAT EXACTLY DOES honour look like?

I had given a seminar talk on Leviathan and, when it was all over, the organiser asked this: 'How do we honour others?' He'd read a lot of the latest books on honour and was frustrated that they all talked so theoretically.

I think the answer, however, is pretty simple. Jesus nailed it when He said: *Do unto others as you would have them do unto you.* The golden rule.

Of course, it's not quite that simple because people's love languages are different, but it's an excellent starting point. Nevertheless in case it seems a bit too theoretical still, let's spell it out some really simple stuff in terms of the needs of the human heart.

LISTENING. Some people have never been listened to; their hearts are desperate for their stories to be known, their names to be acknowledged, their lives to be seen and their personhood to be accepted. About thirty years ago, I used to say, 'Give someone your undivided attention for five minutes and you'll have a friend for life.' About fifteen years ago, it dropped to two minutes. It's often said that, for children, love is spelled T-I-M-E, but I think it's true for many adults too.

THANKING. If someone does something for you, thank them. This should be an obvious common courtesy, but it isn't any longer.

ACKNOWLEDGING. A bit like the last point, but where gratitude is unnecessary. It simply says that you've heard. Don't however have a 'one-size-fits-all' response—there are few things more dishonouring than realising you've spoken about something really important to you and have been fobbed off with a generic dismissal.

RESPONDING. If someone asks for your help, do what you can, state the limitations of your own authority and ability in the matter and then, if necessary, point them to someone better able to assist them further. Do something rather than nothing. Check on the outcome.

QUESTIONING. Delete the phrase, 'You're wrong!' from your vocabulary. It invariably sounds like an accusation and is bound to bring up negative emotional responses from past hurts. Instead try: 'Why do you think that?' or 'How did you reach that conclusion?' This of course will mean you have to practise **LISTENING**. After adequate discussion you might finish with, 'I guess we'll have to agree to disagree.'

Appendix 4

The Number of a Man and also a Beast

YES, IT'S THE INFAMOUS 666. Over time, many people have advanced various theories about the 'number of a man' and, for many years, I tried to steer clear of them all. I regarded it as impossible to decipher with any surety. Nero. Domitian. Henry Kissinger. Adolf Hitler. Peter the Great. John Lennon. The stylised lowercase 'b' logo of a bankcard.

If you're like me, you look at that list and sigh. Deeply. So imagine my surprise when I found an answer I could seriously credit as having fingered exactly the right person. I was reading a poem by Geoffrey Chaucer—actually, truth be told, I was analysing its mathematics—when I became suspicious his line count identified 'the Beast'. Or at least the medieval candidate for the role. But it was an utterly outrageous suggestion. Yet he wasn't the only fourteenth century poet who'd made subtle hints of the same sort.

Still, it was such a stupid idea, I couldn't see how anyone at any time could have thought it. 'They weren't that dumb in the Middle Ages,' I said to myself. 'They knew *better* than this.' And because they did indeed know better, I started to wonder what they really meant. And looking at 666 through medieval eyes, I came to the conclusion they might well have been right.

So, before we *calculate* the Number of the Beast, let's note several things:

First, the number wasn't always 666. The oldest manuscripts show it was originally 616 and, during the second century, those who held to the view it was 616 copped serious criticism. Now, given that Revelation warns so clearly against changing any aspect of the prophecy, there are some points to consider about this variation:

- No one would alter the number without an *extremely* good reason
- 616 therefore is likely to contain an ambiguity that led people to the wrong conclusion
- 666 should clarify any ambiguity inherent in 616
- Nonetheless 616 and 666 ultimately should point to exactly the same answer

The only possible reason for a faithful scribe changing the text, given the extreme curse proclaimed on anyone who did so, was because 616 was exceedingly confusing. However, if it's possible to interpret 666 correctly, then 616 should also make sense.

So, for me, the touchstone regarding any interpretation of the Number of the Beast is that the answer should explain *both* 666 and 616.

Secondly, let's take a quick excursion and look at some selected numbers in Scripture. Not too many because I don't want to bring out any latent anxieties when it comes to arithmetic.

The mathematical structure of the Scriptural writings was of paramount concern to the Jewish people: one of the tasks of the 'scribes' was to count the words, letters, jots and tittles in any scroll to ensure it had been copied correctly. The Hebrew name of this elite group, the 'sopherim', actually doesn't mean *scribes*, it means *counters*. In the days before photocopiers and scanners, the way to ensure the accuracy of a document was to have a method of checking totally independent of reading the words themselves. This was a highly specialised job with a surprising amount of theory behind it.

The Greeks adhered to similar ideas. They had numerical rules for creating plays and poems that modern writers consider unbelievably restrictive and confining. But I love them! (All my books are designed using some of these rules.) For the Greeks, numbers were gods. Platonism, with its philosophy of ideal forms, was infused with Pythagorean mysticism. As far as the Pythagoreans were concerned, a group of ten dots arranged in a triangle and called the 'tetrakys' was the Number of Numbers, Truth Incarnate and Manifest Deity. They also considered it to be the source of nature, the creative principle behind the universe, the Meaning of Meaning, the heart of the Logos.

And by 'Logos', they definitely did not mean Jesus of Nazareth as the Word of God. They meant what we would call the 'golden ratio'. The 'logos' was a mathematical concept. And in John 1:1, it is used in multiple senses—it doesn't just mean *word*, it also means *ratio*. John reflected and affirmed Genesis 1:1, which contains three instances of the golden ratio, while refuting the Gnostic understanding of the Logos. He made this clear because his opening sentence is 17 words long.[127] Now that doesn't mean a single thing today, but to John's Greek audience, they would have been shocked. You simply didn't use 17 to structure polite literature; it had religious overtones for the Pythagoreans who considered it abominable. And as for combining with the Logos with its nuances of goodness, beauty and truth—it was as if John had taken out a sledgehammer to smash a long-revered tradition.

This was a culture where numbers were sacred and some of them were invested with more sanctity than others. One such was 101, which is discussed in the book *Dealing with Python*. Another was 153, the so-called 'measure of the fish' from the geometry of Archimedes. This number is found in the last chapter of John's gospel and it links back to the 17 words of the iconoclastic opening sentence. Also found in both the first and last chapter is the number 496: there are famously 496 syllables in the opening Hymn to the Logos and 496 words in the last scene of the entire gospel.

This handful of numbers is sufficient to show the mindset of the person who used the 'logos', that is the golden ratio or 0.618, as well as 153, 496, 616 and 666 to symbolically highlight the work of Christ and also counterpoint it to the anti-Christ.

The numbers 153, 496 and 666 all have something in common. They are triangular numbers. So is the tetrakys that the Pythagoreans considered to be Manifest Deity. Its four rows of dots arranged in a triangle—1 in the first row, 2 in the second, 3 in the third, 4 in the fourth—add up to 10 dots. So the fourth triangular number is 10.

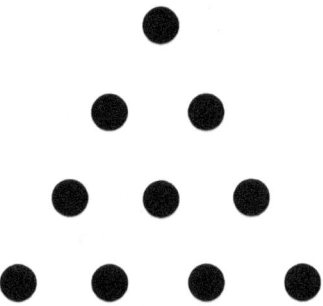

Now if you added more rows to the tetrakys—5 dots in the fifth row, 6 dots in the sixth and so on until you reached 17 rows—then you'd have the seventeenth triangular number. It is 153.

If you kept adding more rows until you reached 31 rows, then you have the thirty-first triangular number. It is 496. (And for any number nerds reading this, it's also a 'hexagonal' number, a 'perfect' number, a 'harmonic divisor' number, a 'centred nonagonal' number and a 'happy' number. And in physics, it's an incredibly important number in superstring theory.) And it's used to bookend the prophecy of Immanuel in the scroll of Isaiah, which is the actual reason I think John used it. Though he was probably taking a golden opportunity to stick it to the Gnostic Pythagoreans amongst the Christian communities at the same time, by throwing those numbers they found despicable—17 and 153—into the mix.

Now add just five more rows of dots beyond this and you've arrived at the thirty-sixth triangular number. And yes, as you've probably guessed, it's 666.

One of the seriously off-putting aspects of arithmetic in both Greek and Hebrew is that their instructions for calculations are ambiguous. Did Jesus say to Peter he should forgive his repentant brother 70 + 7 times or 70 x 7 times? Actually, it's not particularly clear. Some translations say 77 and some say 490 because of this uncertainty.

But this highlights a difficulty. Since we're told to *calculate* the Number of the Beast, what are we to do with 6 and 6 and 6? Add them? Multiply them? What do all these sixes mean? Are they actually to do with the thirty-sixth triangular number? After all, 36 is 6 x 6.

We do have another clue. And it's a really important one. We're told they are the 'number of a man'. But what's that mean? And how does it connect to 616, if at all?

Now, if you decided back in primary school you hated mathematics, you're probably overwhelmed right now. So let me cut to the chase and not bore you with the calculations but just say I believe it doesn't matter what way you slice and dice these sixes, you should eventually arrive at a singular identification.

And that identification is precisely the same one as I pointed out was connected with the number 101 in *Dealing with Python*. As I noted there, Paul used 101 to structure Ephesians: it has a famously convoluted 202-word sentence at the beginning while at the end it features 101 words within the Armour of God sequence.

John, I believe, used different numbers from Paul but with exactly the same intent and purpose. The very fact we can make the same identification from entirely different perspectives is, I believe, confirmation of what 666 actually stands for.

Both John and Paul were adamantly saying that God created numbers, they are not God in themselves; God is the sustainer of the universe, not number or equation; Jesus is the Logos but He is not the golden ratio, instead He is the one who devised it and stamped it on every created thing. And then both apostles get a bit snarky. The subtext of their numerical patterning is this: right, you Gnostics, let those of us who have actually met Jesus make ourselves totally and absolutely clear: He is *not* a reincarnation of Pythagoras! He's the Son of Man, not the son of a man. He's the Son of God, not the son of a number! Understand the difference, you heretics: resurrection—coming back to the same body—is about Christ; reincarnation—being reborn in a different body—is about the spirit of the anti-Christ.

6 x 6 x 6, or 216, was considered to be the number of years between the various re-incarnations of the 'divine'

Pythagoras. Stories suddenly started to emerge with eerie parallels between the deeds of Pythagoras and those of Jesus—there was one about a miraculous catch of fish; the difference being that Pythagoras was a vegetarian, so he let the fish go!

6 was thought to be a 'circular' number because 6 x 6 was 36 which has 6 on the end. If you keep multiplying by 6, you'll always get 6 on the end, proving its circularity since it keeps coming back to itself. In addition, the thirty-sixth triangular number simply pointed to the whole concept of triangular numbers and thus back to the Pythagoreans and their adoration of the tetrakys. If this isn't enough in itself, the Greek version of the name Pythagoras in gematria is said to be 666.

But what about 616? Does it also point to Pythagoras? This is where I'm on less sure ground, because I'm going to have to speculate based on the known facts. However I think it's possible to make a reasonable case. Pythagoras had lived at the same time as the prophet Daniel. In fact, Pythagoras arrived in Babylon as a captive just a few years after Daniel was whisked off from there to Persia. Like Daniel, Pythagoras studied with the magi. We don't know what status Pythagoras reached in their ranks but we do know that, on at least two occasions, Daniel was appointed as chief of the magi. And these astrologer-philosophers knew a thing or two about mathematics: they could solve quadratic equations, for example, and that's the very ability you need to be able to find an approximation for the golden ratio. Moreover, there's a very nifty diagram that's been associated with the magi for forever-and-a-day. It's the five-pointed star called the pentagram. These days the pentagram is associated with satanism and witchcraft—but that's a relatively recent theft. Before the mid-nineteenth century, this star—which is crammed full of lines that intersect in the golden ratio—was called, amongst other things, the 'Seal of God'. And why wouldn't it be? The 'logos' is stamped all over it.

Now, there's always been a tug-of-war over the pentagram. It was not only the 'Seal of God' and at one time a symbol of Jerusalem, but the Pythagorean Brotherhood adopted it as their symbol and allegedly called it the 'number of man'! If that's not a clue pointing to the 'number of a man', I don't know what is.

Now the *Pythagorean Brotherhood*, founded by Pythagoras, has never really ceased to exist. That's what I think those medieval poets were saying.

And here's my speculation. It's based on what we know about the Babylonian magi and their emphasis on 60 as the basis of their number system. They divided a circle into 360 degrees, a degree into sixty minutes and a minute into sixty seconds. Using this information, I believe their approximation to the golden ratio (which is in fact an infinite decimal) was not 0.618 but 0.616.

I'm not just plucking 0.616 from thin air; I believe it is encoded fairly simply in the phrase MENE MENE TEKEL PERES. However, I also think Daniel himself was aware that the more accurate value was 0.618. So, it's my view the Pythagorean Brotherhood used the digits 616 for the mathematical representation of the 'logos', but the Hebrews, following Daniel, used 618. As I've shown in *God's Panoply*, it's clear from Genesis 1:1 that the Hebrews knew of this value and used it to indicate how God stamped His entire creation with what was to become known in later ages as the 'logos'.

My thought is therefore this: 616 was used as the Number of the Beast to point to the Pythagorean Brotherhood and the whole Gnostic movement. It said, just a little bit too subtly as it turned out, that 616 *falls short of the mark* of the more accurate value, 618. To a Hebrew thinker, *falling short of the mark* was a very clear and explicit way of expressing *sin*. It implied a call for repentance to those who were involved in Pythagorean mysticism.

However to Greek thinkers, near enough was good enough. Across the cultural divide of Jew and Gentile, 616 moved from highlighting *sin* to meaning *almost perfect*. It implied the Pythagoreans were on the right track!

Hence why I think it was changed. It was ambiguous. It muddled the whole reincarnation vs resurrection debate. There wasn't a question of immortality of the soul in the early church; it was about what immortality looked like.

Pythagoras has now been dead for around 2500 years. Back in the fourteenth century, he'd have only been deceased for about 1900 years but you can see why I was initially taken aback by the views of those medieval poets. How can someone who has been gone that long be the Anti-Christ? But then it became a little clearer: the Middle Ages experienced a major resurgence of Pythagorean theurgy. Actually it has never gone away and still rears its head occasionally—the last time we saw a major new wave of it was when *The Da Vinci Code* inexplicably became a publishing phenomenon.

Now Pythagorean mysticism has two main arms: one is mathematics, the other magic. One is scientific, the other is religious. One is analytic, the other is occult. Somewhere along the centuries, these two split from each other so today we have atheists who hold to one branch of these ancient tenets and religious seekers who hold to another.

At its deepest core, Pythagorean philosophy is misogynistic. It is anti-woman. This is a really serious problem when Scripture is translated by those who are unknowingly influenced by the west's long cultural heritage of Platonism with its deep interweaving of Pythagorean theurgy. In *As Precious As Pearls* and *As Resplendent As Rubies*, I have looked at Jewish scholarship which delves into the role of women in Scripture. The stark contrast with Christian commentaries is, at times, astonishing. Yet should it be surprising that, when we've welded ourselves to a philosophy with its roots in Python worship, that a hatred of women pervades many institutions—even Christian ones?

> *And I will put enmity between you and the woman, and between your offspring and hers.*
>
> Genesis 3:15 NIV

> *The dragon was enraged at the woman and went off to wage war against the rest of her offspring.*
>
> Revelation 12:17 NIV

The 'woman' here is of course the Bride of Christ. And within our own ranks are those who are aligned with Python, in league with Ziz and complicit with Leviathan. The mesmeric hold of the dragon on some believers' minds has its legal right in dishonour. The intransigence of thought that accompanies this mesmerism leads to a rigidity in institutional structures: the true Body of Christ is flexible, creative and supple but the counterfeit is jointed stiffly and impervious to healing change, just as Leviathan is described as joined and sealed so tightly nothing can get beneath its scales.

We can get all caught up, worrying about the Mark of the Beast or implanted microchips or a global cashless society and allow it to distract us, so we never ask ourselves: what mark is *already* on me that gives Leviathan rights to retaliate against me? What *genius loci* have I aligned myself with through that tattoo? What covenants do I have because of my false refuges? Who or what did I sacrifice to Python in order to get over the threshold into my calling— and am I marked like Cain because of that sacrifice?

Because, at the end of the day, there is a far more important number: 777. This number, as I have shown in the analysis in *God's Panoply*, is encoded within the mathematical background of Paul's description of the Armour of God—

along with a treasure trove of allusions to flowers and gems, priestly garments and nations!

The Armour is the very thing we need to protect us from all the threshold spirits, including Leviathan. It is covenantal; dependent on our oneness with our Bridegroom and the sweet intimacy of our walk with Him.

Ultimately dwelling close to the heart of Jesus, under the shadow of the wings of His prayer shawl, is the only true safety.

Endnotes

1. Leviathan has several heads but I only sensed one.

2. This is an example of what I once dubbed 'counter-symbols'—that instead of a head, you might see a tail. To me, it's almost as if the mind tries to solve a symbolic equation by making use of the same sort of operations used in algebra.

3. In the mythological world, creatures with a stinging tail include the chimera and the manitore. In the physical world, they could also include comets—since going through the tail of a comet subjects us to meteoric bombardment.

4. Tom Hawkins of *Restoration in Christ Ministries* was a specialist in helping believers overcome ritual abuse. His pioneering insights into appealing to the court of heaven are often overlooked.

5. Regarding the spirit of forgetting, see in this series, *Dealing with Ziz: Spirit of Forgetting, Strategies for the Threshold #2*, Armour Books 2018

6. It was a covenant symbol because, during a blood covenant, an animal is cut in half so that the participants can walk through the pool of blood in the centre. By tearing a body shape in half, James was evoking this imagery.

7. http://www.stuff.co.nz/auckland/local-news/manukau-courier/685482/Carved-gateway-opens-at-airport (accessed 11 January 2020)

8. This was the Pool of Bethesda where Jesus healed the man who was paralysed for 38 years. Archaeological excavation has revealed it was outside the old walls of Jerusalem and was a shrine to the healing serpent, Asclepius. For more details, see *Dealing with Python: Spirit of Constriction, Strategies for the Threshold #1*, Armour Books 2017

9. Alistair Petrie, *God's Footprint in Business: Bringing Transformation to the Marketplace*, CHI Books 2019

10. See, in this series, *Dealing with Python: Spirit of Constriction, Strategies for the Threshold #1*, Armour Books 2017

11. This particular word, *support,* is currently used only in *The Message* and *The Passion Translation*.

12. Long before I realised that 'cursing the day' was not metaphorical, I was aware of what may well be a related concept: threshold spirits seem to have more influence on particular days. Specifically days that are associated with the 'New Year', which is of course a threshold in time. It doesn't particularly matter which New Year, any will do, from any culture. This became apparent when I was first working with Janelle, Janette and Janice to help them pass over the threshold into their calling and strange problems would occur for all of them on the same day.

    Although it seems odd that a person can curse a day and rouse Leviathan, I believe that the issue is that, in cursing a day, people are effectively cursing the sea, the natural habitat of Leviathan. In Hebrew, the word 'yom', *day,* is derived from 'yam', *sea*.

13. Stephan Decatur, US naval officer and commodore, 1816

14. Carl Schurz, US senator, 1871. (thoughtco.com/my-country-right-or-wrong-2831839; accessed 25 January 2020) The article at this website goes on to say:

    > In 1901, British author GK Chesterton wrote in his book, *The Defendant:*
    >
    > > 'My country, right or wrong' is a thing that no patriot would think of saying except in a desperate case. It is like saying 'My mother, drunk or sober.' He goes on to explain his view: 'No doubt if a decent man's mother took to drink he would share her troubles to the last; but to talk as if he would be in a state of gay indifference as to whether his mother took to drink or not is certainly not the language of men who know the great mystery.'
    >
    > Chesterton, through the analogy of the 'drunk mother', was pointing out the fact that blind

> patriotism is not patriotism. Jingoism can only bring about the downfall of the nation, just like false pride brings us to a fall.

English novelist Patrick O'Brian wrote in his novel *Master and Commander*: 'But you know as well as I, patriotism is a word; and one that generally comes to mean either my country, right or wrong, which is infamous, or my country is always right, which is imbecile.'

15. If we don't repent of our involvement with Ziz, God will bring upon us suffering and chronic illness along with the death of our children. This is because Ziz and Jezebel are functionally the same spirit—and this particualr consequence of an alliance with Jezebel is spelled out in Revelation 2:22–23.

16. In *Joy Unstoppable*, an audio teaching on Leviathan.

17. My mother also encountered a very similar situation with a Malaysian boy whose grandfather cursed the day he was born.

18. See *Dealing with Python: Spirit of Constriction, Strategies for the Threshold* #1, Armour Books 2017. However, to add a subsequent question to the information in that book, *just why* is a threshold spirit also a spirit of divination? It doesn't matter whether this threshold spirit is Python or Leviathan. What does divination have in common with thresholds? Both, it turns out, are about openings. Thresholds are about doors and gates; divination is about opening our minds to a spirit. Python and Leviathan are encountered on opening a particular kind of spiritual door: ones that are characterised by having an unholy or defiled threshold. This aspect of divination raises, of course, very awkward questions for those who are hugging a particular personal prophecy close over their lives. If Python is blocking the doorway into our calling, how can we be sure that those prophecies we've received are indeed from God and not instead some form of divination? What is the difference? Prophecy is about forth-telling; divination about foretelling. Prophecy is about interpreting pattern;

divination about interpreting signs. Prophecy is about faith; divination about fate. Prophecy is about a call for repentance and turning back to God; divination is about an immutably fixed future. Now if we can't bear to let go of the prophecy, even if it is genuine and legitimate, are we holding fast to the hope it provides, instead of the One who is the Anchor of Hope? Are we using the prophecy as a false refuge? And if that's the case—if it's divination and thus a counterfeit, or if it's the real deal that's become a false refuge, we need to surrender it to God and ask for it to be smashed. And if we resist doing that, we need to ask our heart, why it is that deep down we don't really believe God has something far better?

19. See *Dealing with Ziz: Spirit of Forgetting*, *Strategies for the Threshold* #2, Armour Books 2018.

20. Azazel is the 'scapegoat' and consequently a spirit of rejection.

21. In my previous books, I referred to Belial as the 'Janissary spirit'. Although I was aware it had to have a Hebrew name, I was unable to find it at the time of writing. As it has transpired, 'Janissary spirit' is an excellent descriptor of its behaviour, since it reveals a significant and overlooked aspect of this spirit's agenda: to turn the hearts of the children against their fathers.

22. During this investigation into Leviathan, I wound up following a trail of clues that led to a spiritual entity called Resheph. At first I hoped to include this information in this book but it became soon clear that it would be better to keep the focus on Leviathan to a simpler level, rather than introduce more complexity. Nevertheless, the more I have researched, the more probable I have found it that Resheph is functionally the same as Leviathan, just as Ziz is functionally the same as Jezebel.

23. Robert Bakker, for example, is adamant on this point. In *Leviathan is the Nile Crocodile, Behemoth is a Young Adult African Elephant*, he says: *'*Leviathan and Behemoth are the two most famous monsters in the literature of the Ancient

Near East. Both are described in detail in the Book of Job in the Hebrew Scriptures. Both, repeatedly, have been cited by Young Earth Creationists as dinosaurs observed by humans. However, the anatomy and behavior of these beings, as portrayed in Ugaritic and Hebrew literature, leads to far firmer identifications of the species inspiring the stories. The Leviathan is a surprisingly accurate rendition of the Nile Crocodile, *Crocodylus niloticus*, with the optional addition of six extra heads. Leviathan, in Job, has: powerful jaws armed with great tooth crowns; skull armor that renders hooks impotent; body armor composed of scales, set close together, that repels spears; ventral armor composed of a mosaic of smooth, potsherd-like, convex plates. The most notable behavior is full body *twisting* that churns water into froth—a close approximation of the classic *Crocodylus* "Death Roll". The seven-headed condition connotes other-worldly power and is the rule for the "Twisting Serpent" in Ugaritic sagas, in the Hebrew prophets and Psalms, and in the Apocalypse, aka "Revelation", of the New Testament. Job, who seems closest to eye-witness testimony, restricts Leviathan to single headedness, but does add flame-thrower breath. Interpreting Leviathan as a cetacean is falsified by the jaws, armor and roll. ... Both African Elephant and Nile Crocodile, before the advent of firearms, were such awesome and frightening creatures that their fame spread to many cultures, transforming the living beasts into the supernatural "Chaos Monsters".'

24. Later legends of the Hydra gave it nine heads or fifty heads, which could regenerate and double in number when severed.

25. Ezekiel 29, for example, portrays Pharaoh as a monstrous river-dweller, describing him using the same imagery as that used in Job 41 for Leviathan. However, he is a greatly enfeebled version of Leviathan, able to be hooked, his scales penetrated, and his body broken when leaned on.

26. There are six cataracts along the length of the Nile, thus dividing it into seven sections.

27. Ninurta was the farmer's version of the god of the thunder and rainstorms of the spring. He was also the power in the floods of spring and god of the plough and of ploughing. Ninurta's earliest name was Imdugud (now also read as Anzu), which means *Rain Cloud*, and his earliest form was that of the thundercloud envisaged as an enormous black bird floating on outstretched wings roaring its thunder cry from a lion's head. See: britannica.com/topic/Ninurta (accessed 1 May 2020)

28. chinatour360.com/yangtzecruises/river/flavor/folklore.htm (accessed 26 January 2020)

29. Pronounced tan-ee-fa.

30. And it probably isn't coincidental either that Tangaroa is the godling of the sea; and Tane of the land. Land and sea are enemies in many legends.

31. The seraph in Egyptian mythology was a throne guardian, and was the basically the same as one of the cherubim. This raises the possibility that the seraphim and cherubim are not distinct categories of angels, just as the tannin is not a separate classification from the nahas. freedomfromdelusion.blogspot.com/2014/12/the-nachash-in-garden-of-eden.html (accessed 14 February 2020)

32. The logic is a bit dubious because you can't correctly say, for example, a dog is an animal and a cat is an animal, therefore a dog is a cat. But you can correctly say a terrier is an animal and a dog is an animal, therefore a terrier is a dog. In other words, there's a huge margin for error.

33. Romans 11:29. This is why you see so many preachers and teachers living truly immoral lives, having totally turned their backs on God, yet still operating in a spectacular gifting. God doesn't tell us to look at the gifts to know fellow-disciples; Jesus said that we will know one another by the fruit we display.

34. Crocodile-like or scorpion-like or stingray-like.

35. This may also be symbolised as acid thrown in the face.

36. The Hebrew word for *laugh* 'tsachaq' (starting with the letter samech) rhymes with 'sachaq' (starting with the letter shin) which also means *laugh* or *mock*.

37. However, because it's a fallen seraph, the laughter it provides seems twisted to derision and ridicule. A friend has observed: 'Kids and young people I have known with bad behaviour problems, or who were under the influence of dark spiritual forces, often seem unable to take anything seriously. Far from negative actions coming from dark intense emotions, more often there is laughter and an "I don't care" attitude. Certainly there is a complete absence of any caring about how other people are affected. It's all a big joke.'

38. For more detail on this incredibly complex event, see *Bent World, Bright Wings: Jesus and the Healing of History #2*, Armour Books 2020. Jesus not only marched into the divine assembly and put it on notice that its time of ruling the nations was coming to a close, but He also implanted the church within a spiritual birth process paralleling the timing of human gestation.

39. A seventeenth century work sub-titled *The Matter, Forme and Power of a Common-Wealth Ecclesiasticall and Civil.*

40. Hobbes, to give him his due, seems to have thought it would usher in the Kingdom of God, not fragment society more.

41. Involving 10 volumes of 5000 pages

42. Matthew 7:9 BSB

43. The correspondence between Hebrew 'heel' and the concept of 'choice' is discussed in the first book in this series, *Dealing with Python: Spirit of Constriction, Strategies for the Threshold #1*, Armour Books 2017.

44. Ahithophel is also mentioned in 2 Samuel 23:34, and is said to be the father of Eliam. Since 2 Samuel 11:3 notes that Eliam is the father of Bathsheba, this indicates the extremely strong probability that Ahithophel was Bathsheba's grandfather.

45. A comment repeated many times by John Sandford in his ministry teachings.

46. See *Dealing with Python: Spirit of Constriction, Strategies for the Threshold #1*, Armour Books 2017.

47. See Mark Sayers, *Facing Leviathan: Leadership, Influence, and Creating in a Cultural Storm*, Moody Publishers 2014.

48. This is an evocation rather than a translation. It is based on a rhyme of 'zar' for 'sar', prince, and the common element 'pt' (phath) which often denotes something to do with an opening or a threshold and is indicative of 'pethen', cobra, serpent, spirit of Python.

49. 2 Samuel 21:9.

50. Perhaps her gender is also instructive. In *Farewell, Babylon*, Naim Kattan's memoir of life in the now-vanished Jewish community of Baghdad, he said: 'Muslims used the same word for wife and for honour: ardh. Sensitive to anything that touched the purity of their wives, mothers or sisters, they nevertheless gave in to studied obscenities.'

51. Rizpah also means *pieced together, cooking stone, joined together, pavement* (the only references are to those within a court which may or may not be significant). The same word is used for the coal that purified Isaiah's lips or the coal that the angel used to cook Elijah's breakfast. Rizpah is a devoted mother who lost everyone she loved (her husband, Saul; her sons; her lover, Abner; her nephews; her family). She therefore had no protector. Her name has similar overtones to that of Levi.

52. The analysis in this particular paragraph relies heavily on the work of Robin Gallaher Branch in *Jeroboam's Wife: The Enduring Contributions of the Old Testament's Least-Known Women*, Wipf & Stock 2009.

53. I believe parents often name their children for the unresolved issue in their family line. Several of David's sons had the word *peace* in their name, indicating that the unresolved issue for him was, as God said in explaining

why he could not build the Temple, that he was a man of blood, a man of warfare. Solomon's heir, however, was Rehoboam, a name that was obviously intended to suggest he would *expand* his father's kingdom. But *expansion of the people* is not the only possible meaning that can be derived from Rehoboam. It also encodes 'rachab', one of the Hebrew words for *proud*. It speaks therefore of dishonour, the very quality David never overcame. Rehoboam, like his father before him, was named for an unresolved issue of his family line—even if it was a different issue.

54. The city of Jerusalem—the capital of Judea—was technically in the territory given to the clans of Benjamin. However, Benjamin was all but wiped out by a coalition of the other Israelite tribes. Jerusalem, formerly Jebus, was ruled for centuries by leaders from the very large neighbouring tribe of Judah, starting with David.

55. In my view, each of the threshold spirits treats truth slightly differently. Python plays with truth in riddles and ambiguity. Ziz tears the truth apart by false accusations and bare-faced lies; Leviathan distorts the truth; Rachab spreads out the truth so it is relative and thus wasted; with Lilith, truth is weaponised; with Belial, truth is perverted and inverted so that good becomes evil and evil good; while for Azazel, truth is unimportant. It is apt to be trampled on by one-sided tolerance, must be 'inclusive', not 'exclusive' or rejecting. Of course, there are shifting definitions of what 'inclusive' and 'exclusive' mean.

56. Doubly bent out of shape here: Baal Aliyan, *lord of sources*, is no doubt meant to pun on El Elyon, *lord of lords*.

57. The title of CS Lewis' classic, *The Weight of Glory*, refers to this aspect of glory and honour.

58. See the online etymological dictionary at etymonline.com for details. Once the shift in sense of the element 'lev' from *lightness* to *raise* had occurred, even words like lever *(something to raise a heavy object)* and levy *(to raise an army or raise taxes)* can be considered as part of this grouping. Looking much wider, the original Proto-

Indo-European root meaning *not heavy, having little weight* is considered to form all or part of the following words: alleviate; alleviation; alto-rilievo; carnival; elevate; elevation; elevator; leaven; legerdemain; leprechaun; Levant; levator; levee; lever; levity; levy (v.) 'to raise or collect'; light (adj.1) 'not heavy, having little weight'; lighter (n.1) 'type of barge used in unloading'; lung; relevance; relevant; releve; relief; relieve. (All listed at the website etymonline.com) Lung is particularly interesting because, as a Chinese word, it means *dragon*. And although the following words aren't related in any way, except through rhyme, perhaps reiver (and thus also 'bereaved', originally *having been visited by the reivers*) is also appropriate in relation to the wider English resonances of Leviathan and its activities.

59. He clearly defined it in a way that was very probably influenced by the classic Star Trek episode from the original series: *The Empath*. That television episode influenced a significant percentage of an entire generation in their thinking about empathy, seeing it as truly entering into another's suffering.

60. Williams envisaged groups of believers he called 'Companions of the Co-inherence', who would practice substitution and exchange, living in love-in-God, truly bearing one another's burdens, being willing to sacrifice and to forgive, living from and for one another in Christ.

61. dc.swosu.edu/cgi/viewcontent. cgi?article=1064&context =mythlore (accessed 10 April 2020)

62. See *Name Covenant: Invitation to Friendship, Strategies for the Threshold #3*, Armour Books 2019.

63. There are many others like Gideon who are 'God-namers'. A God-namer is a person who is inspired to give God a name from encountering Him in a uniquely personal way; this is different from God announcing His name as He did to Abram and Moses. The first of the God-namers is Sarah's slave Hagar. Other God-namers are discussed in

As Resplendent as Rubies: The Mother's Blessing & God's Favour Towards Women II, Armour Books 2020.

64. There are other words in Hebrew for *recompense* besides shalom. These include gemul, gemulah, gamla, peullah, temurah, shillem, shillumah, shalam, sakar, saskar, naqam (which has overtones of vengeance), shub and din.

65. From *The Word for Today* by Bob and Debby Gass, published by *Vision Christian Media*. Free introductory issues of this devotional may be obtained (within Australia) from *Vision Christian Media* by phoning 1800 00 777 0.

66. The original course was very informative but it is wise to be aware that, since the founder has died, there are many offshoots all claiming to be the genuine inheritor of the mantle.

67. Also spelled Rahshaf, Rasap, Rashap, Resep, Reshef, Reshpu, Rapha, Repheth and other variants that are not standardised.

68. en.wikipedia.org/wiki/Resheph (accessed 12 March 2020)

69. The Hebrew says 'arum' meaning *subtle* or *wise*. That same word is also used in the previous verse, where it is translated as *naked*. Here is also a double meaning: Adam and his wife were both 'arum'—*naked, subtle* and *wise*—but the 'nachash' was more 'arum' than any other 'living being'.

70. *Heel* in Hebrew also means *if*; and *if* is the iconic religious word in both Greek and Hebrew associated with the spirit of Python. See *Dealing with Python: Spirit of Constriction, Strategies for the Threshold #1*, Armour Books 2017.

71. Genesis 2 and 3 use the name Yahweh Elohim, but both the woman and the serpent, the 'nachash', leave Yahweh out! Since 'Yahweh' is the unique identifier of 'elohim' (which can mean both God and godlings), this is very significant.

72. This suggests the presence of yet another threshold spirit. Passivity is often associated with the spirit of abuse.

73. Lucifer is, in fact, a relatively modern name created during the translation of the King James Bible. Prior to this giving

of a proper name to the *son of the morning* in Isaiah 14:12, this fallen entity simply had the title *light-bearer*.

74. According to Willem Glashouwer, the word 'diabolos' means *scrambler* or *blasphemer*, but also *divider*.

75. Every nation has its own godling. See Exodus 5:2, 12:12, 15:11, 18,11, 20:3, 22:20, 23:13, 32–33, 34:14–17; Ruth 1:15; 1 Samuel 17:46; 1 Chronicles 16:25–26; Isaiah 36:18–20; Ezekiel 28:1–10; Daniel 1:2, 2:11 and 47, 11:36–39; Acts 12:22, 17:18–34; 1 Corinthians 8:5; 2 Corinthians 4:4; Galatians 4:8; 2 Thessalonians 2:4.

76. The word *dragon* comes from 'drakon', meaning *sea serpent*. Dragons are part of the mythology of many countries. A red dragon is featured on the Welsh flag; England's patron saint, George, fought one and Arthurian legend is rife with them; Korea, Japan, Vietnam, India, as well as ancient Greece and Rome, all featured variations on dragons as did the indigenous cultures of Australia with their Dreamings of the rainbow serpent. The rainbow feathered serpent of Meso-America is a relative. The Norse put dragons on the prows of their longships, sometimes hooding them so as not to alert the local land spirits to a coming raid.

77. It also turns up in the name of a goddess, Tanit, though the reasons are not apparent.

78. Thanks to Josephine Lake for noting the word 'Shalom' can be translated as *the Spirit* (or *authority*) *that destroys chaos*.

79. Also Dothan (the biblical location which Joseph reached just before his brothers so savagely retaliated against him for his dreams and his father's favouritism), Dathan, Bethan, Cathan, Matthan, Fintan, and Tangaroa.

80. *God's Priority: World-Mending and Generational Testing*, Armour Books 2017.

81. God's instructions to the Israelites in Exodus 14:2 seem, millennia later, to be just a set of road directions: '*Turn back and camp before Pi-hahiroth, between Migdol and the sea; you shall camp in front of Baal-zephon, opposite it, by*

the sea.' But this is not simply a map; there are allusions to four spirits of the threshold in this verse. In order, they are Leviathan (Pi-hahiroth), Migdol (memory/forgetting), sea (Rachab), Baal-zephon (Python). And that takes no account of the pursuing armies of Egypt. When there is no way forward on a threshold, when every avenue of progress is sewn up and booby-trapped by the enemy, God can still make a way by opening up that which has never been opened before. But it's no coincidence that Numbers 33:7 tells us this fine detail: '*They journeyed from Etham and turned back to Pi-hahiroth, which faces Baal-zephon, and they camped before Migdol.*' Etham is a placename most closely related to the *time of the present*, perhaps *the appointed day*. God has a way through. Sometimes we know, through prophecy or His word what that way through will look like. But when we try to take it in our timing, not His, we wind up retaken as captives by the pursuing armies or smashed against the threshold stones.

82. Isaiah 27:1 NIV.

83. en.wikipedia.org/wiki/Lotan (accessed 25 September 16)

84. Isaiah 27:1 NIV.

85. en.wikipedia.org/wiki/Lotan (accessed 25 September 16) Lotan is the 'mighty one with seven heads'.

86. Strictly Abram, since this was before the name covenant with God when he received the name Abraham. But, in order to not introduce confusion, I will consistently refer to him as Abraham.

87. Some scholars suggest that Lot was, in fact, older than Abraham—even though he was his nephew. Still, it doesn't negate the fact that Lot had benefitted enormously from his association with Abraham.

88. See *More Precious than Pearls: The Mother's Blessing and God's Favour Towards Women*, Armour Books 2016

89. 2 Peter 2:7–8 BSB says: '*Lot, a righteous man distressed by the depraved conduct of the lawless (for that righteous*

man, living among them day after day, was tormented in his righteous soul by the lawless deeds he saw and heard).'

90. Theories about the name of Jericho suggest that it originates in the Canaanite word for moon (*'Yareah'*) or the name of the lunar deity Yarikh, who was worshipped in early times in the city.

91. Generally thought to derive from the Canaanite word 'reah', *fragrant*, Jericho's current Arabic name, "Arīhā', means *fragrant* and also has its roots in Canaanite 'reah'.

92. Although there is no evidence that the *obstinate/hard* connection occurs with Lachish, it does occur with other words such as chazaq (*to harden, to become obstinate, to harden the heart*), qasheh (*hard, harsh, obstinate*), amets (*harden, firm, obstinate*). The other remote possibility is that Taanach, a city name of unknown origin, might be related to 'taanug', *luxury, dainty, exquisite* from 'anog', *soft, pliable, delicate, dainty, effeminate, delight oneself.* These are in turn from 'naga', *touch* (as well as *stroke* and *plague*).

93. Joshua 7:1–26.

94. *Shifting Nations Through Houses of Prayer*, Rick Ridings, Patricia Ridings, CHI-Books 2019.

95. Elizabeth traditionally was visited by her cousin Mary at Ein Karem, *spring of the vineyard*. There the beautiful Magnificat was first proclaimed.

96. The word 'nachash' is also cognate with a term used in relation to Jezebel's utilisation of sorceries. It is 'keseph', *to whisper a spell*.

97. Its other meanings include *stirring, overflowing, inditing*.

98. I am however prepared to be persuaded otherwise, since this all depends on what the definition of *divination* is and its original understanding. The ISV footnotes to Genesis 3:1 say give as an alternative translation to the traditional word, 'serpent': 'Or *the Diviner*; the Heb. word *ha-Nachash* connotes one who falsely claims to reveal God's word; or *the Serpent*; cf. Isa 14:12; Eze 28:13–14'.

99. Genesis 3:6.

100. See *Hidden in the Cleft: True and False Refuge, Strategies for the Threshold #4*, Armour Books 2019.

101. Goliath, who was killed by a rock to the skull, might have a name related to 'gulgoleth', *skull* (though admittedly the text uses 'metsach' in relation to his death). Perhaps there's a relationship as well—prophetic, if not etymological—between the name, Goliath, and Golgotha, *the place of the skull*.

102. Weighing about 85 kilograms or 190 pounds! This doesn't include his helmet.

103. David is from 'duwd' from a root, 'dowd', *to boil* which is also translated *love* and *uncle* or *father's brother*. 'Duwd' rhymes with 'ruwd' *restless, wanderer*. However *boil* can also derive from 'zuwd' which sounds like 'zuwr', *to become estranged, foreigner, enemy*. It is the same as 'duwd' meaning *pot* and *kettle* as well as sounding like 'duwts', *to leap and dance*. It may be related prophetically if not philologically to 'duwr', *ball, circle* (from *heap up, pile, dwell*), or related to 'dowr', *period, generation, dwelling, habitation* and to 'duwach': *rinse, purge, wash, cleanse*.

104. 1 Samuel 28:2.

105. 1 Samuel 16:21.

106. The opening of Matthew's gospel really emphasises this link. It points out fourteen generations from Abraham to David, fourteen from *David* to the *exile* and fourteen from the *exile* to Jesus.

107. 1 Samuel 18:7 NIV.

108. Joshua 15:14.

109. See Footnote 26 in *Dealing with Python: Spirit of Constriction, Strategies for the Threshold #1*, Armour Books 2017.

110. It's true that he doesn't mention confession of sin but he does mention repentance.

111. 1 John 1:9 CEV.

112. 1 John 5:13 CEV.

113. To make it worse, the staff actually symbolised loyalty to God.

114. Told to Pastor Ben Gray.

115. I'm using this spelling consistently in my writings where Scripture translations use 'Rahab'. This spelling variation is a legitimate alternative and is used to avoid confusion with Rahab, the inn-keeper of Jericho.

116. Brown-Driver-Briggs.

117. Perhaps spiritually related to cursing a day and thus rousing Leviathan against a particular person is the Japanese concept of 'ushi no toki mairi', *ox-hour shrine visit*, which refers a ritual cursing of a rival during the hours of the ox (between 1 am and 3 am). See en.wikipedia.org/wiki/Ushi_no_toki_mairi (accessed 14 December 2019)

118. When Maui hauled the stingray which became the North Island of New Zealand up from the seabed, his first cast of his line was foul-snared on Te Whakapunake-a-te-matau-o-Maui-Tikitiki-a-Taranga. His hook fell and fused with the land as Te Matau-a-Maui. His blood remained smeared on the island of Waikawa, the barb of his hook. wairoadc.govt.nz/assets/Document-Library/wastewater-consenting-project/technical-reports/tangata-whenua/Technical-Report-Tangata-Whenua-Worldviews.pdf (accessed 17 June 2019)

119. The issues surrounding the almost wholesale replacement of the word 'Israel' in the New Testament of the Danish Bible are complex ones. After all, it is rightly pointed out that the modern secular state of Israel is not the Israel of the Bible which, to make matters more confusing, was a people group descended from Jacob as well as a largely apostate kingdom during the time of the divided monarchy. New readers of the Bible often find these matters confusing. Nonetheless, in an era of rising anti-semitism, coupled with painful memories of centuries of ill-treatment of Jewish people, it is not at all surprising that contemporary Israelis are suspicious of the textual

changes and the motives behind them, and attribute them to an excessive zeal for replacement theology. The unacknowledged aspect for the Bible translators is that God has placed His name on the land itself, covenanting with land as well as people. biblesocietyinisrael.com/our-statement-on-the-contemporary-danish-bible-2020 (accessed 11 May 2020) www.bibelselskabet.dk/new-danish-bible-2020-and-israel (accessed 11 May 2020)

120. He was also called Te Atua Wera, *the fiery god*.

121. The *first*, with all the threshold overtones and creation of precedent, that implies.

122. This may in fact not be true—some assert this was a false accusation. But if it was, then it came in the first place from other Maori. And certainly Te Kooti Arikirangi and later Rua Kenana Hepetipa (Hephzibah) who both made use of Penetana Papahurihia's legacy saw themselves as members of the Jewish race. In the early twentieth century Rua, calling himself Te Mihaia Hou, *the New Messiah*, built Hiona, that is, *Zion*, on the side of Maungapohatu, a mountain in the inaccessible wilds of the Urewera ranges. His community was known as the *New Jerusalem* and he worked to build his meeting hall from a description of what he thought was the Temple but was in fact the Mosque on the Temple Mount.

123. See: *What's Behind the Ink? The Spiritual Aspects of Tattooing, Piercing and Other Fads from a Christian Perspective,* William Sudduth, RAM Inc, 2004

124. On the healings of history mentioned in these paragraphs (and many more as well), see the series *Jesus and the Healing of History* which, at the time of writing, is comprised of *#1 Like Wildflowers, Suddenly*; *#2 Bent World, Bright Wings* and *#3 Silk Shadows, Rings of Gold*.

125. Jonathan Cahn in *The Paradigm: The Ancient Blueprint That Holds the Mystery of Our Times* connects eclipses with the Shemittah. He is unsure of the meaning of this connection and so am I. However since the Shemittah is connected to

release of debts, release of slaves, to covenant and to times of transition—all of which are part of Jesus' death—it suggests that the eclipse at the time was symbolic of a Shemittah.

126. We make covenants through sacrificing to their entities: sacrificing ourselves, sacrificing others, sacrificing the honour of God. We can also sacrifice to them through the creation of a 'false refuge'—a place of consolation away from God in times of trouble or disappointment. We are apt to realise we have a false refuge if it is overt sin, such as pornography; but we are also likely to overlook it if it seems innocent, such as comfort food or a good book. I was contacted recently by a woman who had discovered in her life the most subtle of all false refuges: prayer. She realised that she actually used the *process of prayer* as her false refuge, rather than God.

127. It's clear that the reason for choosing 17 would be to oppose Gnosticism which was so tightly entwined with Pythagoreanism. According to Plutarch, Pythagoreans would never use 17 because Osiris had allegedly been dismembered into 17 parts and was unable to be properly re-integrated because one of the 17 parts could not be found. John's use of 17 would therefore clearly oppose both Egyptian religion (and Osiris as *'The Resurrection and the Life'*) as well as the Pythagorean notion of re-incarnation. However, a negative reason for using the number does not seem satisfactory to me, unless there was also a positive reason. After a decade of looking for possible symbolic meanings for 17, the best answer I can come up with is that 17 points to 70. Because of the ambiguity regarding arithmetic operations (forgiveness can be rendered as 70 + 7 and also as 70 x 7), it may well be that 'spiritual government' could be symbolised by 10 + 7 or 10 x 7. Certainly 70 occurs in this context many times. Thus I believe—at least at this point until I find a possible alternative solution—that 17 as the ubiquitous 'number of Christianity' used in the gospels and epistles also points to the 'number of the Council of Christ', that is, the Body of Believers as a spiritual government.

www.ingramcontent.com/pod-product-compliance
Lightning Source LLC
Chambersburg PA
CBHW021056080526
44587CB00010B/271